THERE SHALL BE AN INDEPENDENT SCOTLAND

Malory Nye

Other books by Malory Nye

Religion the Basics
(Routledge, 2nd edition 2008, first edition 2003)

Multiculturalism and Minority Religions in Britain
(RoutledgeCurzon, 2001)

A Place for our Gods
(Curzon, 1996)

Time for Change Report
(Al-Maktoum Institute Academic Press, 2006,
co-authored with Abd al-Fattah El-Awaisi)

There shall be an independent Scotland

British and Scottish nationalism after the 2014 #Indyref

MALORY NYE

Perth St Johns Press 2015

Copyright © 2015 Malory Nye

All rights reserved.

ISBN: 1511845775
ISBN-13: 978-1511845779

Printed by CreateSpace, an Amazon.com company

(also available as a Kindle ebook at
http://t.co/AUd8BwrKiC)

CONTENTS

	Preface	5
Part One	British nationalism, Scottish nationalism	
Chapter 1	Introduction: There shall be an independent Scotland	11
Chapter 2	British, Scottish, and English nationalism: The problems of nation and identity in the United Kingdom	14
Chapter 3	What does it mean to be British? why the British may one day learn to be more like the Scandinavians	16
Part Two	Scotland in multicultural Britain	
Chapter 4	'Leftie multicultural cr*p' it was not: but did the London Olympics opening ceremony give us the legacy of diversity that we need?	24
Chapter 5	Multicultural Britain 2.0 is the best answer to Ukip: we need to learn how to live at ease with our diversity	28
Chapter 6	Downton Abbey and the rise of Ukip: soft nationalism and the politics of nostalgia	32
Chapter 7	British nationalism: a love that dares not speak its own name	37
Part Three	Historical reflections	
Chapter 8	The Treaty of Perpetual Peace, 1502	44
Chapter 9	Looking for ourselves in Hilary Mantel's Wolf Hall: the ongoing fascination for histories of Tudors, Stewarts, and the Protestant Reformations in Scotland and England	49

Chapter 10	The declarations made by the city of Perth against the Union in 1707	54
Chapter 11	Eleven reasons why Scotland should remember Henry Dundas: from slave trading to empire building	57
Chapter 12	Scotland's #Indyref: some historic reflections on Devo-max and independence from Britain	68

Part Four — **Getting ready for the #Indyref, September 2014**

| Chapter 13 | The issue with Scottish independence is not 'Yes' or 'No': it is when and how | 76 |
| Chapter 14 | While Cameron pleads for us to keep it in the family, Scotland sings 'I want to break free'... | 81 |

Part Five — **After the #Indyref: There shall be an independent Scotland**

Chapter 15	The day after yesterday (the day after the referendum)	88
Chapter 16	I voted Yes to an independent Scotland… and I look forward to the day when it happens	91
Chapter 17	'Dear Generation Yes': an open letter to the new generation who hoped for Scottish independence	94
Chapter 18	Conclusion: imagine an independent Scotland	98
	About the author	102

Preface: Why I wrote this book

In all honesty, I never thought I would write such a book on Scottish independence.

As someone from an English family (my parents came from the south east, in Essex and Kent), it surprises me that I have felt moved to express my opinions on the issue of Scottish national identity.

I have always thought of myself as British. I spent much of my childhood in rural North Wales. Although I was born in mid-Wales, I grew up with a clear 'saes' (English) identity that I never lost. (Likewise, my English accent has stayed with me through my travels.)

I have now spent much of my adult life in Scotland, first as a PhD student in Edinburgh, and then, after a short return to London in the early 1990s, I have lived in Scotland continuously since 1995 — in Dunblane, Dundee, and most recently in Perth. Perhaps most importantly, my children are all native Scots (even those who were born in England).

And so after this developing process of my life (made up of accidents of circumstances and also a series of choices that have made up my life), I have found myself living through the debate about Scottish independence. This is, perhaps, the most significant political debate that has taken place within the UK nation's three hundred year history.

It has given me the chance… No, it has forced me to think about what the ideas of national identity, of being British, Scottish, English and more might mean, and how these fit together within the jigsaw of contemporary British cultural life. And as I started off in this process, I discovered that it was not enough to talk about being British in terms of nationality and citizenship alone.

Yes, it is helpful to have it defined on a passport that I am more than the sum of my English, Welsh, and Scottish identities. But if I held a different passport then that would not change the issue of being British. And more importantly, a national boundary between Scotland and northern England would not change the immense cultural (and historical) ties between the various nations. We would all still be British, it would just force us to find new ways of thinking about what that meant to us.

In short I have put this book together out of my frustration at the result of the 2014 Indyref. It was a lost opportunity for a political change that would have brought far more benefit than harm to Scotland. But it was also a very important stepping stone on the inevitable path to Scottish independence.

And when that eventually happens, the regional family of nations that is Britain will live more comfortably with each other. Or at least, I hope we can do that. After all, we will all still be British.

Malory Nye
Perth, 23 April 2015

Part One

British nationalism
Scottish nationalism

Chapter 1

Introduction: There shall be an independent Scotland

In the last part of September 2014, I heard a lot of talk about the 'settled will' of the people of Scotland. That is, the assumption that the result of the 18 September Independence Referendum had been resolved, with the 'comfortable' majority vote of 'No'. Thus, many people assumed that the vote had sorted out the issue 'for a generation', and that the people of Scotland were now happy to go back to their normal lives as citizens of the United Kingdom.

As these claims were being made, however, other more interesting things were happening. In particular, the membership of the pro-independence parties (in particular, the SNP and the Greens) saw a very significant boost. For example, the Scottish Nationalist Party membership more than doubled in the month after the Indyref (from around 25,000 to over 50,000), and by March 2015 its membership had doubled again to over 100,000[1]. In contrast, at the time of writing (April 2015) there are predictions being made of a 'meltdown' for the Scottish Labour Party in the 2015 UK general election, largely as a result of the high profile anti-independence role of Labour in the run up to the #Indyref.

It is clear that there is no settled will, and that after 18 September things here in Scotland will never be the same again. Everything is still up for grabs, and my prediction is that the issue of independence will be resolved

---

[1] www.heraldscotland.com/politics/scottish-politics/snp-boost-as-membership-soars-past-100k-mark.1427009904

at some point. The real question is whether it will be sooner or later.

It might take twenty to thirty years, but it will happen. And when it does happen it will be better both for the various parties who currently make up the United Kingdom, and more broadly for the communities and nations of the British Isles and Ireland.

It is with some irony that I have used for the title of this book a paraphrase of the first line of the Scotland Act 1998[2]:

'There shall be a Scottish parliament.'

When the parliament finally held its first session on 1 July 1999, the first Scottish First Minister, Donald Dewar, read out this line with pride. It had been engraved on the ceremonial mace of the parliament.

Dewar himself was a unionist and I am sure that he would not have been too happy for his words to be paraphrased in such a way. But for many Scots the re-establishment of the parliament was a starting point towards the eventual (long term) outcome of an independent Scotland.

The #Indyref took us tantalisingly close to this ambition. Few expected the vote to end with a 'Yes' victory, but many hoped for this outcome.

I was personally very disappointed on 19 September. Along with many others, I had hoped to see the change that needs to occur.

The bleak prospect on view that day, following the announcement of the 'No' victory, brought back keen memories of 10 April 1992, when a Conservative party was re-elected as the UK government in Westminster, even though they failed to have a single MP elected in Scotland.

As I noted on 20 September, the perspective of history was useful to recall. Without the pain of that earlier day in 1992, it is quite possible that later developments under New Labour in 1997 may well have not come about, including the cast-iron pledge for a vote on Scottish devolution that led to the re-establishment of the Scottish Parliament in 1999.

Like many others, I also took great heart from the blog post 'Wipe your eyes, on your feet' by Robin McAlpine on Bella Caledonia[3]. As the name suggested, it was about tough love. We are in the end all like big kids, with the choice of sitting crying about our hurt, or we can look to ourselves, take

---

[2] www.legislation.gov.uk/ukpga/1998/46/section/1
[3] bellacaledonia.org.uk/2014/09/19/wipe-your-eyes-on-your-feet/

stock and move forward, carrying our pain with us.

And this is very much what motivated me to put these papers together in this short book.

When the campaign for the referendum began in 2012, it was clear that it would be historic and highly significant. I did not expect that the result would be close, or indeed I did not think that by the time the vote happened I would be dearly wishing for a Yes outcome of independence.

Like many others in Scotland, I moved a long way during the campaign. It felt like I was part of perhaps one of the most important historical developments of my lifetime. And like the tennis player Andy Murray[4], I felt very uncomfortable with the negative tone of the anti-independence campaign, particularly in its last few weeks.

And what is clear in the outcome of the vote is that the historical process is still ongoing, towards an inevitable result of independence for the small nation of Scotland.

As a scholar of society and culture, my interest is both personal and academic. Being part of this change has made me think closely about the issues of nationalism and identity that I have been teaching in classes for nearly two decades. My primary focus has been on diversity and multiculturalism, which as I show in some of these papers are a significant part of this process.

Most of these papers are presented as they were originally published, in the present tense of that time — either before or after the referendum — and are dated as such to show their historical context. Other papers were written around that same time, but have been edited and updated to the present of April 2015, slightly later after a time of reflection. The debate is going on, and I hope this short book will be a further small contribution to that process.

---

[4] www.bbc.co.uk/news/uk-scotland-29323123

Chapter 2

British, Scottish, and English nationalism: The problems of nation and identity in the United Kingdom

The 'dust' has 'now settled' on the 'No' victory in the Scottish independence referendum. I am proud to say that I voted 'Yes', and like many in Scotland I was disappointed by the result.

Despite the best hopes of the 'No' victors, the debate over Scottish independence will continue for a long time to come. I believe that Scotland will be independent one day, and perhaps the relative closeness of the vote on 18 September has made that more likely to happen within the next generation.

Meanwhile, the Conservative Prime Minister David Cameron's[5] opportunism in turning the 1.6 million votes for Scotland's exit from the United Kingdom into a debate on 'English votes for English laws' did not go unnoticed.

The British myth of invisible nationalism

A very noticeable part of the referendum debate within both Scotland and England was the allegation that independence was primarily a matter of Scottish nationalism, and that such nationalism was otherwise unknown in contemporary Britain (except for in the fringes of Ukip, the EDL, and

---

[5] http://www.theguardian.com/politics/2014/sep/19/david-cameron-devolution-revolution-uk-scotland-vote

BNP).

This is simply not true.

The problem that is at the heart of this debate is that there are competing national identities. These competing identities exist not only *between* the nations that make up the United Kingdom, but at the level of each individual citizen member of those nations.

We are used to a simple idea of nationality. 'I am French', 'she is German', 'we are Chinese', and so on. In such a viewpoint, nationality may be simple and benign, or an over-zealous 'nationalism' that can lead to intolerance, exclusion, and violence.

No one wants to be seen as an over-zealous nationalist.

But in fact, much of the debate about the referendum was about competing ideas of national identity. In many respects, when talking about governance, states, and independence it cannot be helped.

Nationalism and identity

Let's start with the basics.

By nationalism and national identity I do not mean to describe a hard and fast entity. Nationalism is a means of expressing identity, with reference to a 'nation', a country, a wide community that usually contains citizenship and other elements of one's life. But such nationality is also something that exists primarily within individuals' mindsets, their imaginings, in ways in which Benedict Anderson[6] talked about as 'imagined communities'.

This does not mean they are made up and fictional. Nations are real and exist, in fact, because they are shared imaginings that are embedded in everything we do – individually and collectively. Our nation exists in the passport we hold, the history that we remember, and the institutions we are part of – laws, education, security and defence, media, economic and business transactions, and so on. As individuals, we can choose how much we engage with and attach ourselves to our nation. (For example, we can migrate and take up citizenship of a new country, or we can refuse to think of ourselves in terms of such identity).

But in the end, the nation we are part of is determined by factors that exist beyond us. We are largely told what our nationality is – it is written in

---

[6] Benedict Anderson, *Imagined Communities: Reflections on the Origin and Spread of Nationalism, Revised Edition*, London: Verso, 2006 (1983).

ink on our passport, which cannot easily be changed.

However, this works best when the concept of nationality is made clear to us. For example, in the United States national identity is made extremely clear, it is a unitary framework that is constructed institutionally and educationally. The task of 'forging' such national identity in the US has been easier in certain respects, largely because of their fairly unified history (particularly for white Americans) as a nation, founded by revolution and the ideals of liberty.

The United Kingdom as a national 'family of nations'

The challenge for the United Kingdom, though, is that its people's sense of national identity has always had an element of ambiguity. There are competing, overlapping, and partly exclusive national identities within the overall national framework. The potential for this ambiguity is to a certain extent acknowledged by the ambition of the naming of the country, as the United Kingdom. Supporters of the UK see it as a nation that is also a 'family of nations'.

Of course, the UK is currently made up of four different nations: England, Scotland, Wales, and Northern Ireland (sometimes called Ulster by some of its residents). This has been so since 1927, before that (from 1800) it was the United Kingdom of Great Britain and Ireland, including as a 'nation' the whole of the island of Ireland.

Northern Ireland became an entity when its majority elected to remain in the UK instead of joining the rest of the island in independence. The ambiguities of that resulted in the long period of the 'Troubles', from the 1960s through to the late 1990s.

In contrast, Scotland was a distinct sovereign nation before the Act of Union created the UK in 1707. Wales has a strong sense of nationhood – expressed most tangibly in history by Owain Glyndŵr's parliament in Machynlleth in 1404 – but has been an annexed part of the Kingdom of England since 1536. The single united kingdom of the UK does not refer to Wales in either the name of pre-1707 Kingdom of England, or in the various Acts of Union and disunion since then. Perhaps the most tangible formal recognition of Wales as a nation was the Government of Wales Act 1998, which established the National Assembly for Wales.

So, in many people's perspectives the issue of national identity within the UK comes down to those four countries – England, Scotland, Wales, and Northern Ireland. The latter is made complicated by the contested ideas of Northern Irish identity as either Ulster (loyalist/union) or Irish.

In this perspective, therefore, the issue of Scottish nationalism becomes a matter of how much it can be allowable, contained, and tolerated within the larger unity of the United Kingdom – the British nation state. Much of the #Indyref discussion by the English majority within this union has been along the lines that Scottish nationalism is alright, but only up to a certain point. Any further than that, it must be contained, for the sake of the union.

And this is where the other aspect of nationalism comes in, the sort of nationalism that is ubiquitously present, but is so obvious that it becomes almost natural – and so largely unsaid.

The elephant in the room of nationalism in the UK is *being British*.

Competing nationalisms: Scottish and British

The 2014 Scotland referendum was not only about Scottish nationalism. It was equally about the future of British nationalism.

The victors of the referendum (those who campaigned for 'No' to independence and 'Better Together') were British nationalists.

That is largely what the result was: 55% of the Scottish population in 2014 felt their future was safest as British nationals rather than in an independent Scotland nation.

In the UK, Scotland is not a nation-state. It is a part of the nation-state of the UK. The referendum was about asking the question of whether that nation-state should be Scotland or the UK.

But the key issue here is that the 'No' vote in favour of British nationalism occurred despite the voters' largely coexistent Scottish national identities.

This is exactly the point made by Gordon Brown[7] in his eve-of-poll speech on 16 September 2015. The focus of his speech was his assertion of Scottish nationalism as an expression of Britain (and British nationalism):

---

[7] http://www.huffingtonpost.co.uk/2014/09/17/gordon-brown-scottish-independence-speech_n_5834678.html

'This is our Scotland.
'Scotland does not belong to the SNP. Scotland does not belong to the Yes campaign.
'This is not their flag, their country, their culture, their streets.'

From this viewpoint, Scottish nationalism is a part of being British. Or to put it another way, British nationalism can be expressed through the specifics of Scottish nationality.

This was at the heart of the debate over Scotland. Both sides were in favour of Scottish nationalism, but those who were in support of 'No' saw Scottish national identity as best expressed 'through the Union', within the larger context of British national identity.

The significance of this was underlined by the timing of Brown's intervention, and the marketing of his speech as a passionate attempt to 'save the Union'. It was an articulation of British nationalism.

'The vote tomorrow is not about whether Scotland is a nation. We are. Yesterday, today and tomorrow.
'Let us tell the undecided. The waverers. Those not sure how to vote.
'Let us tell them what we have achieved together.'

There were strong feelings on either side, of course, and the breakdown of the votes showed that there are a growing number of people who feel they are Scottish and only that. But even they remain British nationals, inasmuch they remain citizens of the British nation-state.

British and English nationalism

Leaving aside (for the purposes of this particular discussion) the issues of Welsh and Northern Irish nationalism, there are also the even more complicated understandings of national identity in England.

It is often said, with justification, that many English people assume that British identity is the same as being English. This is often the complaint made by other Brits, such as the Scots and Welsh, who are British but not English.

It is at the heart of the development of the United Kingdom, since the time of the Act of Union, if not before. English national identity exists, and is often assumed to be the same as British national identity. After all, until 1999 all parliamentary power in the UK was centralised in London, and London remains the functional capital of the whole nation of Great Britain.

So, we have Scottish and British national identity and English and British national identity. If we try to map them out into a whole, it often creates areas of considerable fuzziness. In short, to be British and Scottish is not the same as to be English and British. It is when these do not sit happily with each other that the 'lower'-level (or alternative) nationalisms (both English and Scottish) tend to come to the fore.

The 2014 triumph of British nationalism

We are left with a result of the 2014 referendum where 45% of Scotland clearly expressed a desire for an independent Scottish nation-state, whilst at the same time the English MP and Prime Minister David Cameron came out of the decision waving the flag of 'English votes for English laws'.

Cameron's reasons for doing so were quite clear, particularly because of Conservative fears (as the historical 'English nationalist party') of losing ground to Ukip, who have been asserting a particular form of predominantly English nationalism (despite their party name referencing British nationalism).

In short, it was British nationalism that won the day in the referendum – whether because of fear or fervour by the Scots who chose this over Scottish independence.

And within the context of the debates, all the main parties proved themselves to be British Nationalist parties, including the Conservatives, Labour, and the Liberal Democrats.

Through these parties British nationalism was given as the seemingly benign antidote to Scottish nationalism. The assumptions that such nationalism is largely invisible and unarticulated do not mean it is not powerful.

In fact, British nationalism proved to have a very potent power.

Its seemingly invisible visibility is what makes it so powerful. It is given the status of a 'force of nature' (how things are) rather than what it is: just another form of nationalism.

This was evidenced to a degree in Cameron's[8] emotional appeals to such a British nationalism as an amalgam of the various nationalities of the union. More particularly though it was the trump card played by Gordon Brown in his last minute speech on 16 September. To do this, Brown used the symbolism of the British nation-state to express the idea of Scottish national identity being understood in the wider (purportedly more inclusive) British nationalism.

> *There is not a cemetery in Europe that does not have Scots, English, Welsh and Irish lined side by side.*
> *We not only won these wars together, we built the peace together.*
> *What we have built together by sacrificing and sharing, let no narrow nationalism split asunder ever.'*

As noted, the sense of nationalism is not only rooted in current institutions. It is built on the historical memory, such as the fighting of wars. This was an echo of the earlier comments of Lord Dannatt[9], former chief of staff of the British army, saying in the Daily Telegraph:

> *'Between 1969 and 2007, Scottish soldiers fought and died to keep Northern Ireland within the overall United Kingdom – more than 100 of them. What was that all about? ...*
> *The United Kingdom is what it is today because of the common commitment of the English, the Welsh, the Scots and the Northern Irish – is it really right that a few thousand [sic] Scots should change the destiny of us all? And in the context of the Scottish soldiers who died to preserve the Union in the face of an armed challenge in Northern Ireland, is there not a democratic opportunity now to preserve the country we love in a better way?'*

Whilst Dannatt was particular about his idea of British unity against the

---

[8] http://www.huffingtonpost.co.uk/2014/09/15/david-cameron-warns-of-a-painful-divorce-if-scotland-votes-for-independence_n_5823692.html?utm_hp_ref=uk-politics&ir=UK+Politics

[9] http://www.telegraph.co.uk/news/uknews/scottish-independence/11093425/Scottish-referendum-Scottish-soldiers-have-died-to-keep-the-UK-together.html

foreign nationalism of Ireland, in contrast Brown's rhetoric failed to note that not all the Irish soldiers buried 'side by side' with the Scots, English and Welsh were part of his common sense of British nationality. Of course, the larger part of Ireland is now the independent Irish nation. Brown also missed out the many British subjects during the First and Second World Wars from India, Africa, and other parts of the empire that were also buried in these graves. Few would suggest that having made their sacrifices and being part of this 'building together' that their countries' subsequent 'splitting asunder' from the UK was the wrong thing to do.

That is, the soldiers of India, Pakistan, and many other Asian and African colonies fought and died 'side by side' with English, Welsh, Irish (from north and south), and Scots during the two great wars. Their countries later achieved independence from Britain nonetheless.

So does 'being together' constitute a nation?

In the modern world, being part of a larger group requires a national identity. There are historians and political scientists who may argue that the larger the union that constitutes the nation, the safer and more prosperous is the nation-state. This is, of course, the debate that is ongoing in the process of European union. It is the basis of the English and British nationalist fears (of Ukip, many Conservatives, and a number of Labour followers) that the creation of a European 'superstate' will transform a wider continental (European) identity into a form of nationalism. That is, British nationalism may itself become subsumed within a European nation-state.

Whilst the United States was able to do this successfully in their portion of the north American continent, they had the advantage of an early start. Likewise Indian nationalism has managed to transform a post-colonial moment into a unification of disparate local national identities. The idea of European nationalism is undergoing considerable resistance by the smaller nationalist units that European history has created – and indeed such local European nationalities were the historical antecedents of the 'modern' concept of the nation and the nation-state that emerged with the 1648 Treaties of Westphalia.

So when we refer this back to the UK, we then have an additional layer of nationalism – not only Scottish and British, but also European, albeit in a relatively gestational stage. It is helpful in this context, therefore, to remember the SNP policy in the 1990s of 'independence in Europe'. This embodied the idea that any common national identity for Scots beyond Scotland should be European rather than British.

In short, the quest for Scottish national independence is located within a matrix of asymmetric and unequal identities. For the 'Yes' campaign, the basis was that Scottish national identity would work most successfully in an independent Scottish nation. The Scottish Nationalist Party was the group that achieved the political basis for holding the referendum, although supporters of the 'Yes' campaign were Scottish nationalists from many other (non-SNP) backgrounds.

On the other hand, the 'No' campaign was based on the idea of 'Better Together' — the sides that should remain together were the various parts of the union of the British nation. In particular, Scotland and the rest. This was a movement that sought to keep the British nation as a whole, and which used much of the symbolism of British national identity.

But it did not feel comfortable with the specific idea — or title — of British nationalism. Although that was what it was.

The small majority in favour of the 'No' vote was a majority for British nationalism.

In the next chapter, I will explore this a little further: in terms of the choices of nationalism in respect of passports, and also by looking at 'Britishness' as something other than a national identity. That is, 'being British' could one day become a regional — rather than a national — identity.

Chapter 3

What does it mean to be British? why the British may one day learn to be more like the Scandinavians

Published on medium.com[10]

11 August 2014

I have always struggled to have a clear idea of my national identity. I was born in Wales, grew up in England and Wales, and I have spent much of my adult life in Scotland. Because of this, it has always felt convenient to think of myself as 'British' rather than anything more specific.

I may soon find myself with a problem. It is possible that the national identity of 'Britishness' will change in the aftermath of the 18 September referendum. If the majority of the people of Scotland vote 'yes' for independence, then which passport will I decide to have? I could keep my UK passport and so become a foreign national in the place where I live, or otherwise I could take a Scottish passport. Maybe I will be able to hold both. Whatever happens, I do not know which I will choose.

Will I no longer be British if I do not have a British passport?

Nationality is more than a matter of identity. Or to put this otherwise, identity is more than a matter of nationality. Sometimes the two overlap quite easily, and we have a passport that states clearly who we think we are. For someone whose family has lived in Scotland for generations then it may

---

[10] https://medium.com/@malorynye/what-does-it-mean-to-be-british-cd6a48fedc49

be an exciting prospect to have a Scottish passport, when they become available. Likewise, perhaps one day we will see the issuing of English, Welsh, Yorkshire, or Cornish passports? Who knows?

Regardless of how the independence vote goes in September, I believe that we are learning a new aspect of our collective identities. That is, what does it mean to be British?

British as a default nationality

For those living in Scotland, Wales, and England, Britishness is their default nationality. And for those like me whose lives and families have spanned the borders of each separate country, it has been a 'national' identity that encompasses several aspects of their diversity.

As a nationality it is rather troublesome, not least because the sovereign nation of the United Kingdom is made up of both Great Britain and Northern Ireland. Not all UK citizens are British, not least, of course, those in the Six Counties who consider themselves Irish (over half a million).

And the legal identity of being a 'British subject' has been used historically in many different ways, including until 1949, any resident of the British Empire. It is still in use for a very limited and dwindling number of individuals who once lived under British colonial rule, in places such as (what is now) the Republic of Ireland (until 1949), the former Malayan colonies of Penang and Malacca (which are now part of Malaysia), and Hong Kong.

All this notwithstanding, the term British citizen technically refers to a citizen of the United Kingdom, that is Scotland, Northern Ireland, Wales, and England.

That will, of course, change if Scotland becomes independent. Citizens of Scotland will become Scottish citizens (but may still remain British citizens if the remaining UK government chooses to allow such dual citizenship with Scotland).

Being British without being British?

So if Scotland becomes independent, and I trade in my UK passport for a Scottish one, will I stop being British? Or more broadly, will Scotland stop being British if/when it becomes independent?

This is where Britishness becomes something more than about

citizenship and passports. Just as it is possible to have a UK passport and be a 'British citizen' without being 'British' (i.e., being an Irish citizen of the UK in Northern Ireland), the identity of being 'British' goes further than pure citizenship.

The idea of Britishness has a history, it was at one point 'invented' (as so many such terms tend to be), making use of historical (largely Greek and Roman) sources to give legitimacy and roots to the concept.

Britishness, and the 'idea of Britain' has been shaped in large part by power, particularly the power of England in relation to the smaller nations of Scotland and Wales, and the forced marriages that took place over the centuries to create the entity that is now the United Kingdom. The sense of Britishness largely came into being with the Act of Union in 1707, when the separate kingdoms of England (including Wales) and Scotland became united as the Kingdom of Great Britain. It was later embedded into a national identity when the further union occurred in 1800, to create the United Kingdom of Great Britain and Ireland.

And not least, the idea of Britishness emerged from defining the nation, culture, and place in a global context – the empire that was British, rather than specifically English. The Britishness of the Empire became the default form of identity of the political configuration that grew out of the United Kingdom of Great Britain and Ireland's global dominance in the nineteenth century.

Britishness, and the idea of Britishness, has also changed and developed. While the former UK Education Minister Michael Gove[11] may have found it easy to talk of 'British values' in the schools of England and Wales, the values of the nineteenth century under that heading were quite distinct from anything we might feel appropriate today.

And whilst Britishness has always needed to encompass a diversity of peoples, for most people (UKIP and BNP supporters notwithstanding) the idea of twenty-first century British identity is rooted in a multicultural and religiously diverse context that has changed almost beyond recognition in the last fifty years. That change has happened — a 'racially homogenous' British identity has long gone. Britishness is now mixed up and heterogeneous.

---

[11] http://www.theguardian.com/education/2014/jun/09/michael-gove-british-values-curriculum

On independence, Scotland will move out of the United Kingdom, but will not move geographically out of the British Isles. The culture of Scotland will not change dramatically from what it was before. Scottish culture has for centuries been a distinctive (and often leading and progressive) branch of British culture. However we may define Scots culture, it shares much with its immediate neighbours to the south, whilst also having strong elements of difference.

In short, although Scots in an independent nation may trade in their British passports for Scottish ones, they will not lose their British culture and identities.

Is Britain the new Scandinavia?

The most useful analogy is probably to look across the North Sea to the distinct national identities of the Scandinavians. The political histories of Denmark, Norway, and Sweden have been linked in various ways, but they have survived into present day collective identities of difference, under the identity of being Scandinavian. This is not a national identity, and unlike Britishness it has never been a basis for such nationality.

But if the people of the various British countries (Wales, England, and Scotland) can see themselves mirrored in their three near neighbours of Denmark, Norway, and Sweden, then the collective identity of being British is not so different from how the people of those countries have lived with being Scandinavian without necessarily being a single political (or national) entity.

Like the UK, the boundaries of Scandinavia have been contested. Finland was once part of Sweden, but is not considered to be Scandinavian in the proper sense. Iceland, the Faroes, and Greenland all have close cultural and historical ties with Scandinavia, but are more properly considered as part of the group of 'Nordic countries' rather than as Scandinavian. Scandinavia has seen a single currency, and sporadic attempts at political union, but has broadly settled into three independent nations sharing a common (more regional and broadly cultural) identity.

For me, this answers the issue of my identity. I may eventually hold a Scottish passport, based on longevity of residence in Scotland. I may see my 'roots' as being primarily English, since both my parents originated from the south east of England. I also have a deep affectual relationship with Wales, where I lived for much of my childhood.

And because I come from the family of nations that make up the British Isles, I have no problem with thinking of myself also as British. That does not need to be a national identity, but rather something that describes much more than what is printed on my passport.

It will be interesting to see how well the rest of the English learn to live with the idea that Britishness is not something that comes from a political union within the British Isles, but is an identity freely chosen by its diverse people.

The term 'Great Britain' may have resonances of an enforced union, led by the dominant England as it expanded its political influence.

But that does not prevent the idea of 'being British' having a less politically charged nuance, describing a family of equals rather than serving as the template for a global empire.

When that happens, it is likely that the idea of being British – in its diverse, multicultural, and progressive sense – will be attractive to most of the inhabitants of this small group of islands.

Part Two

Scotland in multicultural Britain

Chapter 4

'Leftie multicultural cr*p' it was not: but did the London Olympics opening ceremony give us the legacy of diversity that we need?

Published in the Huffington Post[12]

30 July 2012

The 2012 London Olympic games were born in the melting pot of multiculturalism. As we were reminded on Friday (27 July 2012), the tragedy of 7/7 happened on the day after the announcement of the success of the London bid. The London games arrived in 2005 with the London bombings. Thankfully, we have come a long way since then.

The rationale for the games had within it the recognition of the need for a legacy of inclusion and diversity. As the 7/7 bombings showed us, we have a lot of work to do to ensure that legacy is successful. This is a huge responsibility for us to hand over to future generations.

For me, this is a major part of what multiculturalism is about. It is not about counting the 'non-white' faces in the pageant, or where they had been placed. It is about working on the process of understanding who we are, and what we can become. I think that was one of the things that Danny Boyle was up to in his gloriously self-indulgent take on how to subvert the concept of an Olympic opening ceremony.

---

[12] http://www.huffingtonpost.co.uk/malory-nye/leftie-multicultural-crp-_b_1716402.html

I must confess I missed the show on Friday night. I wasn't invited, of course, but I missed my seat in front of the TV, as I had carelessly found myself in hospital. Thank heavens for BBC iPlayer and Youtube[13], the moment will now last forever. I must stress I didn't find time to jump and somersault on my hospital bed[14], sadly there were too many wires and sticky pads to allow me to join in. But like Mr Boyle I pay tribute to the great doctors and nurses of our NHS, and Ninewells Hospital in Dundee in particular.

So what was the opening ceremony about?

The comments by Aiden Burley MP[15], who tweeted as he watched the event that it was 'leftie multicultural crap', have been shot down quickly by his friends and foes (not least Boris Johnson).

All well and good. It was not crap.

But it portrayed workers and bosses, and it portrayed diversity in various ways. To a degree it was historically revisionary — not radically so (and certainly not marxist). And it appears the Queen still enjoyed it, once she'd recovered from her parachute jump[16].

The imagery of the ceremony was rich and provocative. I am sure that scholars will spend many years trying to deconstruct and analyse the messages of the event — of what it tells us about Britain in 2012.

What did the imagery of the dancing, drumming industrial revolution[17] actually mean? Was Mr Bean's performance[18] representative of a collective indifference to high pomp and ceremony, or did it tell us of a more general apathy to the contemporary national political and social processes? Answers on a postcard please... or in a conference paper abstract?

But the question I cannot help asking is whether this is a representation of multiculturalism to applaud or one to critique? Or both? As one of the commentators said about the music, what is most interesting is not what was included but what was not.

To put this another way, did it show us an inclusive vision of our

---

[13] http://www.youtube.com/watch?v=4As0e4de-rI
[14] http://www.youtube.com/watch?v=ReJjvlipXpM
[15] http://www.theguardian.com/politics/2012/jul/28/olympics-opening-ceremony-multicultural-crap-tory-mp
[16] http://www.youtube.com/watch?v=1AS-dCdYZbo
[17] http://www.youtube.com/watch?v=7QL_uG2GSZo
[18] http://www.youtube.com/watch?v=CwzjlmBLfrQ

country, or was it simply an enjoyable and complex representation of diversity today?

It did show me a lot of what I know of my country: of history, of class, and diversity. Also youth, technology, music, and communication. It was great to see. It was a spectacle that pushed many boundaries.

But I am sorry to say that it was a mainly English vision. The Olympics are in London, yes. And London is England, for sure. The ceremony was first and foremost a celebration of the city, not the wider country (of countries).

To have choirs from Ireland, Scotland and Wales singing on windy causeways, beaches and castle crags said volumes — they were outside the stadium looking in. And yes, Emeli Sande is Scottish, as was JM Barrie, and JK Rowling has become a native (as I have too). But the imagery was very much a local English set of images.

Funnily enough the contemporary youth culture bridges that cultural gap more than the historical. Status updates and grime music are not local to any part of the country (everyone of a certain age is certainly 'bonkers!'). There is a lot of shared culture, but there are differences too, and not only in the kitsch tartan-shortbread-tin symbols. For heaven's sake, has Mr Boyle not seen 'Trainspotting' (lol!)?

When there was so much other diversity showed, it is a shame that there was not much to show the rich national differences of our country, as well as our points of communality.

And where was the question of religion? Apart from in the awkward moment when the camera focused in particular on a Saudi female athlete as Jacque Rogge, the IOC President, welcomed the women members in every national team. I could not feel any point of contact with Islam and Muslims as part of Britain. This is a nit-picking point, perhaps, but one of huge significance given the 6/7 origins of the London games.

The most recognisable sign of Islam in Britain today — the hijab (women's headscarf) — was only seen on the heads of the international competitors. Why not have it worn by the home performers too? Do we think that there are no young Muslim women into Dizzee Rascal?

I am a firm believer in the idea of a multiculturalism that is inclusive and not separatist. As some writers have argued, multiculturalism requires a strong national identity, that brings all people in to a common space. If anything, the processes of multiculturalism need to allow us to have our differences and also to feel a sense of sharing an identity too.

The former prime minister Gordon Brown (from Scotland, of course) nodded towards this, with his attempt to encourage the question of 'Britishness'. His agenda is now long gone, but the questions still remain. Events such as the Olympic ceremony make bold, memorable, and lasting representations of such a vision — and will probably have significant influence for years to come. But we are not there yet.

So, let the games begin!

Chapter 5

Multicultural Britain 2.0 is the best answer to Ukip: we need to learn how to live at ease with our diversity

Published in the Huffington Post[19]

28 May 2014

It is now (2014) two years since the London Olympics showed the world London's central message of diversity and multiculturalism — not just for the games, but also as its ongoing legacy. In doing so, it sent that message on behalf of the whole UK. The games, as well as the world's focus, is now moving on to Brazil, a country that successfully lives with diversity built into its national identity.

The run up to and now the developing aftermath of the May 2014 local and European elections in the UK have left quite a bitter taste in the mouths of many. The seeming victories (largely outside of London) of the UK Independence Party (Ukip) have been based largely on emphasising the worries and concerns of a substantial part of the ethnic majority of the UK.

These worries really do exist, that immigration, and the cultural diversity that comes from such change, both need to be resisted. Ukip have built a platform by arguing for the reinstatement of the UK as a self-confident and successful nation which can apparently be achieved through returning to a monochrome sense of identity. For Ukip, migration, diversity, and

---

[19] http://www.huffingtonpost.co.uk/malory-nye/ukip-election-diversity_b_5394771.html

multiculturalism (whatever that might mean) are a challenge to such self-confidence and need to be resisted.

The transformation of Humpty Dumpty

This is all happening against the background of one of the greatest historic challenges to the make-up of the UK. That is, the 18 September vote for independence in Scotland that could possibly cause the 'decapitation' of the UK (geographically if not economically or politically). Whether Ukip like it or now, what is very largely the English independence party (David Coburn notwithstanding) may find themselves fighting their corner in a much reduced United Kingdom after 24 March 2016.

When the process of devolution started for earnest in the 1990s, Michael Forsyth[20], the then Conservative Scottish Secretary (a role some saw as the chief colonial officer for Scotland) made the comment that if devolution was to happen, then it would not be possible 'to put Humpty Dumpty back together again'. It would be done, and could not be undone.

Scots who are pro-independence (the 'yes' camp) welcome this, of course, and many see the 1997 referendum as an inevitable part of the process of dismantling Scotland's role in the UK. To remain with the 'Humpty Dumpty' analogy, the creation of the super-Scottish omelette has required the breaking of some eggs.

In short, the process of devolution of much of the UK's political power over Scotland back to the country — in some form or another, whether that be independence or devo-max — was inevitable once the 11 September 1997 vote delivered a 'yes-yes' result. The main issue has been how Scotland, and its near neighbours, should make the most of the opportunities offered by these changes, rather than recriminations over whether or not devolution should have happened.

Britain has transformed already and we can't go back

Ukip's ideological platform is based on a fundamental error. Their rallying call against immigration and diversity is similarly about trying to put Humpty Dumpty 'back together'.

Diversity in the UK (including in Ukip's Essex back yard) is well and truly a fact-on-the-ground. Britain (little and great) has been a diverse country since the 1960s, for more than half a century. What has been

---

[20] http://www.bbc.co.uk/otr/intext/Forsyth24.11.96.html

debated during that time is how it could and should live with that diversity. Every government during that time has had to make some positive contribution to those debates — some more than others. It is reassuring to hear that Tony Blair[21] is keen to defend his party's own positive contributions in this regard.

The main Ukip message seems to suggest that 'send them home'[22] is the only thing that will solve this 'problem'. As Lenry Henry was saying back in the 1980s, the only answer he could give to such a suggestion was to 'go back' to his Black Country (West Midlands) roots.

Going home is being here. Plain and simple. If Humpty Dumpy is a white, racially homogenous UK, then that is well and truly 'broken' (or transformed). We are a diverse nation. The question is instead how we live with that.

There have been many predictions that both the Conservatives and Labour will move to the right in the next year, out of fear of the impact of Ukip's anti-multiculturalism. I am not sure if this is the necessary and 'politically correct' route to ensure electoral success in 2015. (I am also encouraged by Mehdi Hasan's[23] comments last year, here in the Huffington Post on the topic of immigration, which I came across as I was writing this.)

The need for a positive approach to multicultural realities

If we are going to focus on the longer term (i.e., beyond the next election), the argument needs to shift away from the politically easy spectres of scapegoating and fear of loss (jobs, identity, and country). There is a much more pressing need to shift the debate onto how the UK is multicultural, what that diversity means, and how for several decades it has been a source of enrichment.

I believe that kudos would go to the party that plays the 'multicultural card' in a positive way, to point out that we are all multiculturalists now. Britain is (or at least should be) a nation that is at ease with its differences

---

[21] http://www.theguardian.com/politics/2014/may/27/tony-blair-labour-take-on-ukip-immigration-eu

[22] http://www.telegraph.co.uk/news/politics/ukip/10503755/Ukip-politician-defends-comments-about-sending-all-immigrants-back-home.html

[23] http://www.huffingtonpost.co.uk/mehdi-hasan/immigration-public-opinion-mehdi-hasan_b_2818180.html

(national, political, economic, ethnic, religious, and other).

Whichever party comes out of the next general election in the winning position should take a lead in helping to define more clearly how a diverse, multicultural Britain (/England) can live more at ease with itself. This is not an issue to run from, but instead we need to recognise that diversity is now (and has been for a long time) a vitally important element of what makes the country what it is.

It is also what will give us the competitive edge that we need to succeed in the globalised twenty-first century. A successful multicultural policy is aligned to economic development, national security, and all the other issues that will all figure high on the agenda of the next election.

Multicultural Britain 2.0

Such a multicultural perspective is not about celebrating diversity, preaching tolerance, or looking to 'recognise' others. It is instead, about acknowledging the diversity of stakeholders in the national debate. It is about the right for people and groups to be different on their own terms, so long as there is also a common ground of identity where all can feel comfortable. It is about acknowledging the challenges of diversity in an attempt to take us beyond the issues of community v. community, identity v. identity, us v. them. It is about *us and us*, together with our differences.

Any political party that can articulate this sense of acceptance, of a social and national wellbeing in the midst of its diversity, would earn the right to govern, and would indeed find itself with an electoral mandate to do so.

It would be nothing more than helping us to accept the realities of today, rather than falsely promising a return to the long gone days of empire and ethnic homogeneity.

Chapter 6

Downton Abbey and the rise of Ukip: soft nationalism and the politics of nostalgia

Published in the Huffington Post[24]

7 October 2014

I must confess that I am a fan of Downton Abbey. I still recall the shock and pain of the Christmas 2012 episode (spoiler alert... when Matthew died), and love the silliness of Julian Fellowes' re-imagining of this long gone era.

When viewing the show last week, it came as something of a revelation to me that the gap between the present series (5) in 1924 and when I was born is shorter than the time between my birth and today. Did the world (in particular England) change so much more between the 20s and 60s than it has from the 60s until now? I am not sure.

But I am now worried about the programme, seriously worried.

Downton Abbey is, in fact, a form of soft nationalist porn that can probably be blamed for the unfortunate rise of Ukip.

I know I should have realised this before.

The incredible power of state media

It has commonly been remarked that the rise of Hindu religious nationalism

---

[24] http://www.huffingtonpost.co.uk/malory-nye/downton-abbey-and-ukip_b_5940194.html

in India[25] came about largely due to the production by the state Indian TV company (Doordarshan) of serialisations of the Hindu religious epics of the Ramayana and the Mahabharata[26] in the late 1980s and early 1990s.

These epic productions revolutionised TV consumption across the sub-continent. When they were broadcast each week, on Sunday mornings, whole communities would come to a standstill, as they gathered around their TVs (often publicly shared) to watch the Hindu religious narratives played out. Very often the TV sets themselves would be garlanded in honour of the stories and the characters they embedded.

And it is certainly true the rise of the pro-Hindu BJP (the Bharatiya Janata Party) and Hindu religious nationalism came about in the wake of this social phenomenon. The recently elected BJP Prime Minister Narendra Modi owes his position (and the power he wields through his party) to the catalyst of these Doordashan religious epics.

Until the early 1990s, the BJP was a minor party. We cannot underestimate the power of national television to instil into diverse peoples (across a nation) a simple narrative about what their lives mean, and what their country means to them. India is a very large country, it is the size of Europe, with cultural and linguistic diversity to match. It also has a very large non-Hindu population (mostly Muslims). The role of the religious epics underlines the power of the idea of nostalgia about a simple religious Hindu identity.

We may step back from this, shake our heads, and say that Downton Abbey is not like that. It is just another ITV period drama, surely?

'Downton Abbey is harmless fun': soft nationalism between consenting adults

But Downton Abbey is perhaps the nearest that we can come to a contemporary story about British national identity (that is, what we would like it to be).

It is obviously about the English aristocracy — the Earl of Grantham (Hugh Bonneville) and his dowager countess mother (Maggie Smith) — and how that aristocracy struggled in the early twentieth century to forestall

---

[25] http://www.amazon.co.uk/Politics-after-Television-Nationalism-Reshaping-ebook/dp/B001G8XG7Y/ref=sr_1_1?ie=UTF8&qid=1412599683&sr=8-1&keywords=Politics+after+Television%3A+Hindu+Nationalism+and+the+Reshaping+of+the+Public+in

[26] https://www.youtube.com/watch?v=1fxwSd0AhEk

the decline that finally hit home a few decades later. Both Grantham and his mother are shown as the fiercest of traditionalists, but also willing to adapt as and when to maintain their privilege. It brings in a wider narrative, though, with Grantham's American wife (Elizabeth McGovern) and the brief use of Shirley MacLaine as his mother-in-law (in series 3).

We also have echoes of the Empire as an ever-present background — Grantham's brother-in-law Hugh (Peter Egan) takes up the role of Governor of Bombay, in India, and most recently we have the character of Simon Bricker (Richard E Grant) who has 'wintered in Alexandria' (in British occupied Egypt). Interestingly, the house itself (Downton) is placed in northern England (somewhere near Ripon in North Yorkshire), even though the building that is used for filming is in fact Highclere Castle in Hampshire.

An ongoing part of the narrative is the character of Tom Branson, who starts as a (below stairs) chauffeur, but has an affair with one of Grantham's daughters. They marry but then she dies in childbirth (oops, sorry there should have been another spoiler alert there). This leaves the former chauffeur as a part of the aristocrat family, with all the class awkwardness that involves. Added to that, however, is his Irishness — he is not British, and proud of it, but has to learn to struggle with becoming part of the British ruling class. This means the couple are caught up in the Irish struggle for independence, and it leaves Branson as an ongoing critic (from within) of British national privilege.

But alongside this aristocracy we have also the success of Downton as telling the other story — the 'downstairs' to the upstairs of the great house. A collection of servants, including butlers, valets, housekeepers, ladies' maids, footmen, cooks, and others give the story its depth. It is in these characters that most viewers have the chance to see reflections of themselves.

These ordinary workers square-off the circle of the Downton universe. They help to portray the microcosm of the house as a picture of the wider world in which it was placed. And in these servants we see something of the (often unrecognised) diversity of that world, including clandestine homosexuality, Scots, unmarried mature women, and rape under cover of 'gentile behaviour'.

The character of 'Mr Bates' stands out in particular, the valet to Grantham, having formerly been his 'batman' in the army — trying to live true to his values, and do the right thing. In order to do so, we feel we know (without being shown) that he has taken revenge for the rape of his wife by pushing the rapist in front of a car in London. He is a man of goodness and honour, but with a dark side.

In short, Downton Abbey is about nostalgia. It is a form of soft nationalist porn.

It presents to us a country that we feel we know, even though that country is a long way from where we now live.

The world of Downton is a place in which we feel quite at home, even though we would never really want to live there.

A country re-united by nostalgia

It tells the story of David Cameron-type aristocrats, but in a wider England that includes northern (and Scottish and Irish) characters. Its main narrative is of a society divided by class, but united by its common purpose.

Of course, there is nothing 'wrong' about TV forming national identity. It happens all the time, in all countries. Sometimes it happens in easy to observe ways, sometimes it is more subtle. As the anthropologist Thomas Hylland Eriksen[27] has observed, even the nightly weather forecast is a form of everyday nation building — it gives us a nice straightforward representation (i.e., a map) of the extent of our nation.

And nationalism (and national identity) is not fixed and unchanging. How a nation thinks about itself changes constantly.

British nationalism has been going through a lot of changes recently. The recession has taken its toll on our sense of who we are and what we should be. And of course the Scottish independence referendum has brought to the fore questions about the extent to which the United Kingdom is 'better together' or not. This did not begin in August 2014, it has been an ongoing debate since at least 1997, with the rise of the devolution of power through the various parts of the United Kingdom.

British national identity is an ongoing process. And as I highlighted in the previous chapter, the idea of being British has changed extensively with the social changes of inward migration. Whether we like it or not, multicultural Britain is diverse, and our national identity will reflect this —

---

[27] Thomas Hylland Eriksen, *Ethnicity and Nationalism: Anthropological Perspectives*, Pluto Press, 2013 (1993).

unless we succumb to the frightening forces of ethnic purism.

And this is where Nigel Farage and Ukip come into the story. It is Ukip that seems to be donning the nostalgic mantle of the supposedly benign Britishness that is reproduced (or produced) in Downton. The appeal of Farage is the idea that somehow we can reverse time and go back to those 'happy days'.

The world of Downton is one of British fairness seemingly at its best. It is a world in which mild prejudices (against gays, Catholics, African Americans, change) are regrettable but still very forgivable.

It portrays a time before the immigration of the second half of the twentieth century, of a time when Britain had real power, and when being in Europe was about fighting imperial wars not dealing with EU regulations.

This is the hard core of the soft nationalism of Downton Abbey. The programme is not (as far as I am aware) a deliberate agenda to reassert a view of Britain that is at odds with the present day reality.

It is the politics of nostalgia in full force.

And it is a potent weapon in Farage's attempt to refight Mr Bates' battles of honour and decency, on behalf of his country (England and the UK) and its people.

Which now leaves me feeling rather uncomfortable about escaping to this world on Sunday nights.

Chapter 7

British nationalism: a love that dares not speak its own name

During the months around the #Indyref, I heard a lot of talk about the importance of being British. There was a real fear that this would be lost if Scotland became independent.

And yet paradoxically there are very few people who consider themselves British nationalists. For most this is an ugly idea, associated with far right xenophobia and bigotry.

Like many people, the Scottish independence referendum made me think deeply about my sense of being British. It has left me feeling quite uneasy about my Britishness. This distinguishes me from 55% of the Scottish electorate, together with the majority of the people in England and other parts of the UK. Most citizens of the UK are British nationalists, although they would probably be reluctant to use that term.

If Scotland had chosen independence in September 2014 I believe that being British could have become something different from a national identity (see chapter 4). I have argued that Britishness could become a form of regional identity, something akin to the Scandinavian identity of the Nordic countries. That is, an identity that is not linked directly to passports, governments, and taxation.

I still believe Scotland will one day be independent, but in the meantime British national identity has proven to more powerful.

I recently wrote a blog for the Huffington Post about the idea of British nationalism within the context of the UK Independence Party (Ukip) and the popular TV show Downton Abbey (see chapter 7). Controversially, I have suggested that the rising popularity of Ukip is a result of the nostalgic imagining of British nationalism as portrayed in the Downton series.

The politics of nostalgia in Downton harks to an idea of Britishness that is clean and simple. This is very attractive to many in the face of the contemporary challenges of Euro-scepticism, multiculturalism, and Scottish claims for independence.

In reading the comments on that blog, I seem to have hit a raw nerve with some readers. I have variously been accused of living in a bubble, being on drugs, and of insulting voters because of this link I suggested between Downton and Ukip.

But I must plead that my argument was not so much about whether the viewing of Downton on Sunday night then makes someone vote Ukip the following Thursday. Of course, in the 'real world' there are many other factors as well as the ones I have highlighted.

To take a different example about the power of media, the rise of Scottish nationalism was encouraged by the film *Braveheart* in 1995. Braveheart did not cause devolution – many other factors were instrumental, particularly the Thatcherite economic policies of the 1980s, the political reaction to the Poll Tax fiasco in Scotland, and the mainstreaming of political devolution through the Scottish Constitutional Convention. But on one level, Braveheart spoke a very powerful message about Scottish national identity, and continues to do so.

My comments about Downton are not intended to demean or insult Ukip and their supporters. For me, Ukip stands largely in an area that has previously been claimed by a large body of Thatcher's English supporters, and also most likely supporters of the early Blair. It is, very clearly, an important political constituency for any party or group that wishes to hold office in Westminster.

And this constituency is largely focused around the interplay between English and British nationalism. It is predominantly English, but is expressed through an identity of Britishness. In many respects it holds Englishness and Britishness as interchangeable (give or take a few quarrelsome Scots and others).

It is no accident that the name of the party that is claiming this ground is the UK Independence Party. In effect, that means Ukip is the 'British nationalist party' – in comparison, for example, with the Scottish

Nationalist Party. It avoids that name for obvious reasons, after all the BNP already exists.

And while the SNP now broadly reflects the focus of Scottish politics as a left of centre party, Ukip reflects the political interests of middle England (outside of London), which is right of centre. Being a nationalist party does not entail being neo-Nazi, although those parties that have claimed such nationalism for Britishness or Englishness have tended to be fascistic in some form (i.e., BNP and EDL, and Mosely's earlier British Union of Fascists).

Ukip's political base comes largely from a portion of formerly Conservative voters, but also from Labour voters – as did Thatcher's support in the 1980s. Such English/British nationalism straddles over the class boundaries in this respect.

The main issue at stake here is not about Downton Abbey, as a TV show or as a modern nationalist myth.

It is instead that British nationalism is very alive, and it is indeed thriving.

It was British nationalism that was chosen in the Scottish independence referendum (as a nation that was 'better together' than in separate parts).

I say this not necessarily to criticise such nationalism. Personally I would have liked to see a vote for Scottish independence, and I believe that it will happen one day. As I highlighted earlier, I see Britishness in terms that are not nationalistic. I do not see the advantages of a united British nation – particularly as so many British people (nearly half of Scots) are unhappy with the union.

But British nationalism is here to stay. Whether it is expressed in Tory, Labour, LibDem or Ukip terms, there are many people in the UK who are fervent British nationalists. Most of these people are English, mainly because the English make up the large majority of UK citizens, and because much of Britishness is linked to English national identity.

And although the term British nationalism usually conveys far-right tendencies, such nationalism (like Scottish nationalism) can in fact be either left or right of centre, and it can be exclusive or inclusive. British nationalism is not solely right wing anti-immigration and anti-multiculturalism.

British nationalism can also be about multiculturalism and pro-diversity. A small example of this is the British nationalism expressed in the London

Olympics Opening Ceremony in July 2012 (chapter 5). The message was clearly about portraying a lasting legacy of diversity for the city of London, for England, and for the UK.

As James Bloodworth[28] noted about the #Indyref debates, such an image of an inclusive Britain was somehow lost in the clamour of unionist politicians (of all parties) seeking to convince Scots to remain part of the nation. And as another commentator Jessica Elgot[29] highlighted, Scottish nationalism has been deliberately and explicitly about inclusion and diversity.

For as long as we have British nationalism, I hope that such inclusiveness is built into the debates about what it entails. Britain is a country that has become diverse, and a strong national identity should involve an engagement with its own differences.

Both the Conservative and Unionist Party and the UK Independence Party proclaim clearly their British nationalism, but both tread softly around the term itself.

For as long as Ukip claim the main mantle of British nationalism there is the fear that such nationalism will be expressed and understood as exclusive and potentially racist. Ukip should clarify their position in this respect, because if it does not then Ukip will be encouraging the idea of British nationalism as xenophobic.

I am by no means a British nationalist. But I live within the British nation and so have a vested interest in it remaining a peaceful, tolerant, and progressive country. In that respect, British nationalism needs to be recognised and defined by all parties that have a stake within it.

That is, there is a pressing need for the definition of a British nationalism and identity that is at ease with diversity, in all its forms.

---

[28] http://www.independent.co.uk/voices/comment/the-better-together-campaign-is-selling-the-wrong-britain-9724176.html
[29] http://www.huffingtonpost.co.uk/2014/06/12/scotland-independence-referendum_n_5488582.html?utm_hp_ref=tw

Part Three

Historical reflections

Chapter 8

The Treaty of Perpetual Peace, 1502

Over half a millennium ago, the kings of Scotland and England swore oaths to ratify a 'Treaty of Perpetual Peace' between the two independent countries.

According to its terms, the treaty would be in force

> *'from this day, henceforth, in all future times, and between [the two kings] and their lawful heirs and successors. We wish to be bound together by this legacy which shall be legitimately passed on to our successors as a true, sincere, whole and inviolate peaceful friendship.'*

It is with some irony, perhaps, that this treaty was broken within just a decade (and so became to a large degree defunct). King James IV of Scotland, one of the signatories, invaded northern England in 1513 in support of Scotland's other international obligation, the Auld Alliance with France. England and France were at war, and so Scotland also had an obligation to support France, hence King James taking this opportunity.

In fact, it is also quite ironic that when King James swore the oath of the peace treaty, in Glasgow Cathedral in January 1502, he initially read out the oath as swearing peace with France — not England. He had to restate the oath, giving the proper name to the country to which he was committing Scotland to a relationship of peace. Such was the nature of international politics in the sixteenth century.

It was not only the Treaty of Perpetual Peace that was ill-fated. King

James led his army into the Battle of Flodden Field on 9 September 1513, against an English army led by Thomas Howard, the Earl of Surrey. King James died, the last British monarch to lose his life on the battle field, together with over 100 of the Scottish nobility and around 10,000 Scottish soldiers. It was a very significant defeat for Scotland.

At the time, Scotland had been struggling to retain its independence from England for more than two centuries, since the time when Edward I of England attempted to include Scotland within the empire that he carved out from the British Isles. By the early sixteenth century, Wales was already largely annexed to England, and the process of bringing Ireland under English rule had been under way for a considerable time.

The sixteenth century was going to prove a time of significant turbulence for Scotland with respect to English dominance. It began with the signing of the Treaty of Perpetual Peace in 1503 and ended in 1603 with the accession to the English throne of the King of Scots, James VI — who became James I of England — thus uniting the two thrones, although not at that point creating a single united kingdom.

Indeed, the two events are related, since it was the marriage of King James VI's great grandmother Margaret Tudor (the older sister of England's King Henry VIII) to the Scottish King James IV in 1503 that formed the basis of peace treaty. The descendants of that marriage eventually took over the monarchy of both England and Scotland.

This was not the first time that the ruling English and Scottish royal families had inter-married. James IV's great grandfather (James I) had married Joan Beaufort in the previous century, who was the granddaughter of John of Gaunt, Duke of Lancaster — who founded the House of Lancaster and so was a distant forebear of King Henry VII.

Margaret's father, King Henry VII of England had taken the English throne by force just fifteen years before in 1485. This was when he defeated King Richard III in the Battle of Bosworth, near Leicester and in doing so brought largely to a close the English civil war between the houses of York and Lancaster. In establishing stability for himself and his dynasty, Henry VII preferred to act more as a diplomat than a conquering warlord, and thus sought a strong alliance with Scotland through the treaty — and through the marriage of his daughter with the Scottish king.

By the time that the treaty was in place, Henry's own Tudor dynasty was looking more precarious, due to the death in 1503 of his elder son and heir,

Prince Arthur, leaving only one son (Henry) and two daughters (Margaret and Mary). Of course, the son Henry went on to become the infamous Henry VIII, whose multiple marriages were largely motivated by an obsession with furthering the dynasty. Despite this, the older Henry's prescience of marrying his daughter Margaret to the Scottish king proved to be the means by which his royal line succeeded. Henry VIII produced three monarchs in the next generation (Edward VI, Mary Tudor, and Elizabeth I), but none of them produced a child to continue the line.

In the end, the inheritance of the English throne went through the line of Henry VII's daughter Margaret rather than through her brother Henry. Margaret's son James V fathered the daughter Mary (Queen of Scots), who in turn was the mother of James VI and I.

This eventuality was even reflected on at the time of Margaret's marriage. King Henry VII's advisers suggested to him that England might see the day when a Scottish king could claim the crown of England.

Henry had obviously given this some thought already, as according to the chronicler Polidorus Virgillius, the king said

> *'if such things did happen (which God forbid they do), I believe that our realm (England) would receive no damage from this. For in that case England would not be added onto Scotland, but Scotland would be added onto England, as to the most noble head of the whole isle. For at that time, that thing that is least is used to be joined onto that thing which is the greatest... Even as when Normandy came under the power of our English forebears.' (Translation by John Leslie[30], The History of Scotland, 1561, p.69).*

His son, Henry VIII obviously had different views on this possibility. It was the issue of succession that troubled him most, and motivated his need to annul his son-less marriage to his first wife Catherine, and his decision to marry several times after that.

Henry VIII had two daughters (Mary by Catherine and Elizabeth by Anne Boleyn) and eventually a son (Edward) by his third wife Jane

---

[30] http://books.google.co.uk/books/about/The_history_of_Scotland.html?id=GJQuAAAAMAAJ

Seymour. He clearly did not feel that a daughter would suffice as a successor monarch to him, although both daughters did eventually take the English throne after the death of his only son. And, of course, the younger of them became Queen Elizabeth I, who has generally been considered more successful as a monarch than her father. Unlike her father, Elizabeth chose to ignore the succession game, as she famously did not marry — leaving her succession to fall by default to her clear (but unnamed) relative in Scotland, King James VI.

Through the time that Henry VIII was causing upheaval in England due to his decision to annul his first marriage and pursue the woman who became his second wife, he could have taken an alternative option. At that time, in the late 1520s and early 1530s, his sister's son King James V was in the position of being a likely heir to Henry. If he had succeeded at that time, then he would most likely have followed the script set out by Henry VII, that is to take up the throne of both Scotland and England, and rule Scotland by proxy from London (as his grandson Jame VI did seventy years later).

Obviously Henry VIII did not wish this to happen, and instead he studiously avoided naming the Scottish James V as a likely successor. At that time, Henry's illegitimate son Henry Fitzroy may well have become king (despite not being legitimate). This did not happen due to Fitzroy's death in 1536, which was followed soon after by the birth of Henry's only legitimate son Edward in 1537, who immediately became the heir to the English throne.

As it happened, James V himself died in 1542, five years before Henry, and in the aftermath of a Scottish defeat at the Battle of Solway Moss — in which James himself did not fight. James was succeeded by his only surviving legitimate child, his daughter Mary. As well as the title of Queen of Scots, she also inherited her father's claim to the English crown, which remained current due to the absence of a male successor to Henry after his son Edward died in 1553.

In the end, Mary only reigned in Scotland for six years, before she abdicated (by force) in favour of her infant son James in 1567, and spent the remainder of her life in England as a captive of Queen Elizabeth — due to her potential threat as a Catholic with a claim on the English throne.

And so, it was Mary's son James who eventually united the thrones of Scotland and England, when he succeeded Elizabeth on her death in 1603.

By that time the idea of a 'Treaty of Perpetual Peace' had largely disappeared in favour of a more outright merger between the two nations. It was, however, the treaty that had paved the way for the unification of the two crowns.

Chapter 9

Looking for ourselves in Hilary Mantel's *Wolf Hall*:
the ongoing fascination for histories of Tudors, Stewarts, and the Protestant Reformations in Scotland and England

Published on medium.com[31]

21 January 2015

A BBC TV adaptation of Hilary Mantel's Wolf Hall is airing tonight (21/1/2015). The timing is quite remarkable for me.

I have just finished reading the first of these books (Wolf Hall). When I began it, the week before, I had no idea that a TV version was on the cards, let alone imminent.

If I track back just a little, I have been exploring ideas around the Reformation for a few months, and I discovered Mantel in that sweet, quiet spot between Christmas and New Year.

My particular interest is what happened in Scotland, particularly around Perth in 1559, when John Knox[32] famously preached in the parish kirk of St Johns. In response, the 'rascal multitude' ran amok and pulled down four ancient monasteries in the city[33].

---

[31] http://medium.com/@malorynye/looking-for-ourselves-in-hilary-mantels-wolf-hall-9e4852e91439

[32] https://archive.org/details/reformationscotl00knoxuoft

[33] Douglas WB Somerset, 'John Knox and the Destruction of the Perth Friaries in May 1559, *Scottish Reformation Society Historical Journal*, 3

For most Scots, that was 'a good thing', because the country was established as a Protestant nation soon afterwards. It happened almost overnight: one minute Catholic, the next Protestant[34]. And only a few executions and martyrs to show for it.

Of course, the story is a lot more complicated than that — particularly if you throw in the romanticism of Mary Stewart, who soon after returned as the Catholic Queen of the Protestant Scots. This was not such a good thing, particularly for Mary, who literally lost her head over it all.

The outcome, though, was the birth of Mary's son James from her second marriage (with the grandson of Henry VIII's sister Margaret Tudor). Hence the young boy, who became King James VI of Scotland, was also the great-great-grandson of King Henry VII of England. This was enough, during troubled times of succession (after the death of the childless Queen Elizabeth) to secure him the throne of England, and so to become King James I of England.

At his accession in 1603, the thrones of England and Scotland were united, through the merger of the dynasties of Tudors and Stewarts. James became known as 'the wisest fool in Christendom', who managed to live through the Gunpowder Plot in 1605 (troublesome Catholics), the Gowrie Conspiracy in 1600 (troublesome Scots in Perth), as well as starting the plantations in Ulster and the founding of Jamestown in America.

The rest, as they say, is history.

So, when I was making this trawl through history, I came across the fascinating figure of Thomas Cromwell, the 'low born' chief minister to King Henry VIII, and the second most powerful man in England in the 1530s.

Without Cromwell, it can be argued, the English Reformation would have been very different.

It is curious in itself that England went through the process of reforming more than a quarter of a century before their neighbours in

---

(2013), 1-34,
  https://www.academia.edu/4592918/John_Knox_and_the_Destruction_of_the_Perth_Friaries_in_1559

[34] Stephen Mark Holmes,' The Scottish Reformation was not Protestant ',International journal for the Study of the Christian Church, 14(2), 2014, p. 115-127 (DOI:10.1080/1474225X.2014.930598),
  http://www.tandfonline.com/doi/full/10.1080/1474225X.2014.930598#.VL6__3uPaT0

Scotland. That was not for want of trying, since King Henry tried to drag Scotland kicking and screaming into his reformation in the 1540s, with what has come to be known as the 'Rough Wooing' of Mary, Queen of Scots. That is, English armies invaded Scotland a number of times to take the infant (Scottish) Queen Mary by force and marry her to the infant Prince Edward (Harry's son and heir, who eventually became the sickly and short lived King Edward VI).

If that had been successful, then the crowns of England and Scotland would have merged half a century earlier than happened, and Henry's episcopalian and state-run form of reformation would have been imposed on Scotland. It has been argued by some that the Scottish Catholic Cardinal Beaton — often seen as an enemy of the reformation due to the brutality with which he dealt with reformers — in fact managed to preserve Scottish religious independence from England, and thus (unwittingly) allowed the reformation in Scotland to have a much more Calvinist and thus Presbyterian flavour.

That is not to say that the Scottish reformation was unrelated to reform in England. The timing of Scotland's turn (1559) coincided with the return of a Protestant queen in England (Elizabeth) after the short but anti-Protestant years of ('bloody') Queen Mary. Indeed, it was English troops that helped to counter the forceful pressure of the French Catholic support for the Scottish monarch. At that time, Scotland was caught between the ties of the 'Auld Alliance' with France or the hoped for relationship of 'Perpetual Peace' with England. In 1560, Scotland became Protestant. In 1603, the Scottish crown was joined with England.

But amid all these details, I still can't help asking one of the central issues of Wolf Hall: That is, why did the reformation happen?

And why did it take the form it did in England?

It is very easy to point to Henry's need to divorce his first wife Catherine, the daughter of the Spanish Ferdinand and Isabella. The Pope would not give him the divorce, so Henry stuck his fingers up at the Pope.

But, as Mantel herself shows with eloquence and humour, the issue for Henry was not divorce.

It was that Henry felt the marriage was not valid in the first place, as Catherine had first married his older brother Arthur. When Arthur died in his teens, Henry not only inherited the status of heir to the throne, and thus the crown, but also Arthur's widow. Twenty years later, in retrospect (and without a male heir) Henry felt that second marriage was an abomination.

The split with Rome was not, therefore, simply a matter of Henry finding a way to regularise his sex life. He had already strayed beyond his marriage — he had an illegitimate son, Henry Fitzroy. In the succession struggles after Henry's death, Fitzroy could have become King Henry the Ninth. That this did not happen was because of his early death in 1536, not because of his illegitimacy.

Panning out much wider, we can perhaps argue that the reformation had to happen. There is the (Protestant) populist view that the Catholic church was too much of a spent force, that it needed to reform.

Certainly, there was much that needed to be improved. For example, post-reformation Scotland saw a certain amount of redistribution of wealth once the monasteries were closed (or destroyed). For example, in Perth lands from the ex-monasteries were endowed by King James to a new hospital, run by the parish. The aim of universal education was to a certain degree put into practice. The Bible was made available in the vernacular. The stranglehold of the clergy was replaced by a new system — some may say it was an improvement.

The reformation was, however, as much a social movement as it was a political change. It was about new technologies changing the way in which people learned and thought. This is conveyed well by Mantel, with her reflections (through the character of Cromwell) on the tracts and publications of the new thinkers — the heretics/Protestants.

Despite the best efforts of the state and the church across Europe to stop this, the easy distribution of printed pamphlets on the new religious ideas (along with new Bible translations, such as Tyndale's) became an unstoppable force. It was the circulation of such texts in Scotland for several decades that made the Scottish reformation much more of a ground-up revolution than in England.

As we see today with publications such as Charlie Hebdo, when there is the technology to 'publish and be damned' then there are often people who are willing to risk death to do so.

The 1520s and 30s were a time of immense change in western Europe. The largest power of the time, the Spanish Habsburg empire, was busy fighting the Ottoman Turks in the east of Europe whilst also plundering the New World (in what is now Mexico, southern America, and Florida) for whatever treasures they could find. The Portuguese in the meantime were taking control of the eastern spice routes in the Indian Ocean and opening up southern and south-east Asian markets and territories for conquest.

In the wake of this, the Spanish (Catholic) Dominican friar Batholomé de Las Casas was asking the question of how Christendom should deal with the native peoples of America, the 'Indians'[35]. From his first-hand experience, the expansion of the Christian world into America left a long and nasty trail of blood and oppression. He polemic against such colonial violence eventually led to the famous debate of Valladolid, in Spain, where he put his arguments against the classical thinker Sepúlveda, for whom the Aristotlean idea of 'natural slavery' could be applied to the people from whom the Spaniards were seizing the American lands and resources.

It was a debate that continued down the centuries, until eventually Protestant reformers (such as Wilberforce and eventually Abraham Lincoln) grabbed this nasty nettle of European exploitation.

In the end, the reformations happened across Europe because of particular circumstances that made reform and political and social change happen rather than internal rejuvenation. It was largely because of figures such as Thomas Cromwell that these became the 'Reformation' that we know.

It is possible that it could have been different, if the circumstances had been different. We only know what we know — and it is helpful for every generation that we have narratives such as Mantel's to help us remember and reinterpret such pivotal moments.

The story itself is ongoing.

After all, why do we want to remember this?

What do we see of ourselves in the reflections of Cromwell and King Henry when we scrutinise them so closely?

---

[35] Bartolomé de las Casas, *A Brief Account of the Destruction of the Indies*, http://www.amazon.co.uk/gp/product/B004UJRUD2?psc=1&redirect=true&ref_=oh_aui_d_detailpage_o01_

Chapter 10

The declarations made by the city of Perth against the Union in 1707

When reading through a late nineteenth century history of the city of Perth by Samuel Cowan (Perth, the Ancient Capital of Scotland), I came across the following citations of declarations made by the city's Town Council at the time of the Act of Union in 1707.

I think they largely speak for themselves.

It is interesting that Cowan saw the usefulness of reproducing the Town Council's unhappiness with the Act of Union, but made no comment of his own in his history on these materials.

Cowan, Chapter 19[36]

'In 1706 the union of the Parliaments in the reign of Queen Anne occupied great attention at Town Council meetings, so much so that no less than two petitions were sent from Perth to London against the Union.

'These petitions are interesting reading, and represent in clear and unequivocal language the feeling that existed on that great national question. The first petition from the Magistrates and inhabitants was as follows:—

---

[36] Samuel Cowan, *Perth, the Ancient Capital of Scotland*,
http://www.electricscotland.com/history/perth/vol2chapter19.htm

> 'That the Magistrates, Town Council, and inhabitants of Perth having seen and considered the articles of union now before Parliament, in which, among other things, it is agreed by the Commissioners of both kingdoms that Scotland and England shall be united into one kingdom and that the United Kingdom be represented by one and the same Parliament;
> 'We after mature deliberation are fully convinced that such a union as is proposed is contrary to the honour, interest and fundamental laws and conditions of this kingdom and to the Claim of Right and to the 3rd Act of Her Majesty's Parliament of 1703; and inconsistent with the birthright of the peers, rights and privileges of the Barons and Burgesses, and may greatly endanger our Church government and bring insupportable debts and obligations on the subjects of this kingdom.

'Second Petition.

> 'The Address of the Magistrates and Council of Perth for themselves and in name of the whole other burgesses and inhabitants thereof.
> 'Humbly Showeth,—That we having seriously thought upon the important concern of the union of the two kingdoms as contained in the articles now published, we think it our duty humbly to offer our thoughts:
> 'This albeit we sincerely affect peace and a good understanding with our neighbours of England. Yet the concluding of a Union as proposed and moulded in these articles is prejudicial to the true interest of this kingdom tending to the destruction of our venerable constitution, independence, sovereignty, and all its rights and privileges, to every person and society within the same especially that of the Burghs: and to shake loose the government of the church as by law established and endanger our religion. For the defence of which this place has on all occasions signalised itself: and to put trade, the great interest of the burgh, under the heaviest burdens, taxes, and impositions without any Parliament to hear and help us, except that of the British one whose interest as we may perceive will never dispose them to favour our prosperity where they can pretend but an imaginary loss by our gain,
> 'Therefore we humbly and earnestly supplicate and confidently expect that your Grace and the Estates of Parliament will not conclude such an incorporating Union so destructive and dangerous to the nation in all its liberties, sacred and civil: but that for the satisfaction of Her Majesty's

subjects ye will be pleased so to settle the state and condition of this nation that our religion, the government of the church as now by law established, the sovereignty and independence of the kingdom, the rights and being of our Parliaments, due regulation of trade with encouraging cases of the duties upon it may all be so firmly established and secured that it may be put beyond danger of subversion or trouble in time to come.

'(Here follow signatures.)

Chapter 11

Eleven reasons why Scotland should remember Henry Dundas: from slave trading to empire building

It is remarkable how history has largely forgotten about Henry Dundas, the First Viscount Melville.

After all, the New Town area of Edinburgh is dominated by his statue, raised up 140 feet high on a column in the middle of St Andrews Square. And there are three streets in that same area named in honour of him and his family (Dundas Street, Melville Street, and Melville Crescent).

Dundas was a major political figure of his time, in the late eighteenth century. He was a close friend and ally of William Pitt the younger, and they were in government together through the British loss of the American colonies, the growth of the new empire in Asia, and the Napoleonic wars.

So why should we remember him? Perhaps we should just allow his memory to disappear into the obscurity of history.

He was man who came from a background of privilege. During his lifetime he exercised considerable power – in both his private and public life – and not always for the benefit of others. In the last part of his life he was involved in a public scandal that could have led to his imprisonment.

But he was also very much of his age, and his life tells us a lot of about the world that he lived in. Remembering Dundas helps us to understand a little bit more about how modern Scotland and Britain was shaped at a very significant time in its history. And Dundas' life is a reminder of the many skeletons hidden within British history – in particular, the ambivalent legacy of Britain's shameful history of slave trading.

So here are 11 reasons why Scotland should remember Henry Dundas:

1. Dundas was a dominant figure in late eighteenth politics in both Scotland and the United Kingdom

Henry Dundas was a very powerful political figure during the 1790s and in the first few years of the nineteenth century. This was a time when Britain's international power was transformed and then consolidated. Britain had recently 'lost' the Thirteen Colonies that had declared independence in 1776 as the United States and the Independence War finally ended with British withdrawal in 1783.

So this was a time when Britain turned its attention to the building of a new empire in Asia, particularly in India. Dundas held office as Home Secretary, War Secretary, chief secretary for India, and eventually the First Lord of the Admiralty. He was for nearly two decades a very close adviser and ally to the Prime Minister, William Pitt.

He was therefore involved in many political decisions of great historical consequence, including the expansion of British interests in India, the reconstruction of the navy that enabled Nelson to win Trafalgar, and the incorporation of Ireland into the United Kingdom.

His role was always one of a practical political fixer, rather than an ideologue. Dundas himself believed that Pitt could not have governed in the way he did without Dundas' own ability to deliver the votes and the support, in the house of commons and further afield.

He was a man of privilege, but not considerable wealth — indeed he was successful in losing a lot of money during his lifetime, as his impeachment was based on his inability to prevent those who worked for him considerably mispending public money. In many respects he was similar to the figure of Frank Underwood in the TV drama House of Cards — that is, the pursuit of power was of far more interest to him than the pursuit of money. Unlike Underwood, however, he did not seek the highest office, he was more content with wielding the significant (whilst largely absolute) power that came with being the lieutenant to Pitt.

His relationship with Pitt was in fact notorious — they were very regular drinking buddies. The story goes that they had both consumed rather a lot of wine one evening when they were called back into the house of commons. Pitt found difficulties, saying to his friend Dundas that he could not see the speaker. Dundas replied that he had no such problem seeing the speaker, in fact he could see two of him.

Dundas was not a member of any political party, and indeed he was known to change allegiance across party lines to further his political career. But due to his close relationship with Pitt, and the length of their partnership, he had an important role in the establishment of the Tory political tradition.

2. Having such a dominant role, there are numerous figures of his era, such as Walter Scott and Robert Burns, who have commented on him

It is quite surprising Dundas has become so forgotten. Having the position and influence that he had, we have on record many comments from influential figures of his time. Sir Walter Scott was a close friend of Dundas' son, Robert (who became the 2nd Viscount of Melville, and is also honoured with a statue in Melville Street in the western part of the New Town).

Following the news of Dundas' death in 1811, Walter Scott described 'Lord Melville's noble intellect' as having a 'brilliant acuteness' and said that

> *'it shall be my prayer to God that, in my very subordinate walk, I shall never be found altogether [unworthy] of the regard with which Lord Melville honoured me'*

Dundas supported and engaged with Adam Smith, being one of the first to read his book *The Wealth of Nations*, and introducing it to William Pitt.

Robert Burns in his poem titled *Ballad on the American War* on British politics named Dundas, describing him as: 'damned auldfarran' (old fashioned and behind the times) and 'slee Dundas' (crafty)

The writer James Boswell, who knew Dundas from their days together at the University of Edinburgh, described him (half jokingly) as a 'coarse, unfettered, unfanciful dog'.

William Wilberforce once said that 'Dundas was a loose man' which made him consider Pitt's relationship with Dundas 'unfortunate'. However, he also remarked that although people often 'thought him a mean, intriguing creature... he was in many respects a fine warm-hearted fellow'.

William Pitt wrote in 1794 that he considered every act of Dundas as 'being as much mine as his'.

3. He was the last peer of the realm to have been impeached – although he was acquitted of the charges against him

This came about due to financial irregularities during his time as Treasurer of the Admiralty, in particularly some clearly dodgy transactions made by Alexander Trotter, involving transferring sums amounting to £15 million pounds from the treasury to his own accounts. It was never clear the extent to which Dundas was aware or not of what Trotter was doing, since Dundas himself refused to speak in his own defence at the impeachment proceedings. The impeachment was heard in 1806, with his chief critic being Samuel Whitbread, the son of the founder of the English brewing company.

Dundas' acquittal from the impeachment did not completely exonerate him, and he retired from much of public life after it had been completed.

4. He inherited his wealth and estate from his wife who he later divorce and disinherited, preventing her from ever seeing her children again

Dundas married his first wife, Elizabeth Rannie, in 1765. Through the marriage, Dundas took ownership of Elizabeth's considerable family wealth — including the estates of Melville Castle near Dalkeith (south of Edinburgh) and around £10,000. He did not have any real personal income of his own, and so much of what he came to rely on (in both land and money) came from this marriage.

Dundas' life took him more and more away from home, particularly after his move to London — since Elizabeth remained on their Scottish estate at Dunira near Crieff. When she had an affair with a man called Captain Faukener in 1778, Dundas' response was to divorce her immediately.

Thanks to the divorce laws of the time, their divorce was resolved fully in favour of Dundas, as the husband. As a result of this, Dundas kept her family wealth and property, and Elizabeth was estranged from her four children, who she never saw again, even after Dundas' death (she lived to the age of 97, dying in 1847). The one consolation from this story is that Elizabeth went on to marry Faukener after her divorce.

These were harsh times for women, as exemplified by Dundas' behaviour towards Elizabeth.

5. He succeeded in diluting William Wilberforce's bill for the abolition of the slave trade in 1792, which in effect delayed this for 15 years

By the 1790s there was a considerable political movement in London for the abolition of both the transatlantic slave trade and slavery itself (particularly the enslavement of Africans in north America). This was led by the reformer William Wilberforce, who introduced a bill in 1792 seeking to abolish the slave trade, that is the shipping by the British of people taken from Africa across the Atlantic.

Dundas had considerable political power and leverage in Parliament, and so was in a pivotal position when it came to the passing of the bill.

At the time Dundas' intervention in this respect was considered to be favourable to the bill — that is, he managed to mobilise enough support within parliament for the bill to be passed and for a decision to bring an end to the slave trade. This was a considerable achievement in itself, and it is hard to know if it would have passed without Dundas.

But Dundas' role in this respect was more complicated, since the price he extracted from the passing of the bill was to add a slight amendment to it that in fact delayed the ending of the Atlantic slave trade by as much as 15 years.

Dundas did not directly oppose the Bill. Instead, he was politically astute enough to propose support for the bill with a seemingly agreeable amendment. He cannily inserted a simple word into the bill, which gained it enough votes to be passed into law. That is, the abolition of slave trading (not the owning and abuse of slaves) in British jurisdiction would occur, but by Dundas' efforts this would occur 'gradually'.

This was a delaying mechanism, that we can only think in hindsight was an attempt to prevent the inevitable occurring at some point.

What it meant in practice was that full abolition of the trading of slaves did not happen until 1807, 15 years after Dundas put in his amendment. That is, by promoting the 'gradual' abolition, Dundas allowed the trading (and kidnapping) of slaves to continue for a full fifteen years.

My rough quantification of Dundas' amendment suggests that because the abolition did not happen until 1807, around half a million people were kidnapped from western Africa and taken across the Atlantic to the West Indies and America by the British. Estimates put the slave trading by the British at that time at somewhere between 10—15,000 per year, which during the period between the 1792 and 1807 Acts amounts to between 450—600,000 people.

6. In contrast, as an advocate in Edinburgh he successfully represented a former slave (Joseph Knight), and won for him the right to live in freedom in Scotland

At an earlier stage in his life, in 1777, while practising as an advocate in Edinburgh before moving to London, Dundas was the legal representative in an unusual case. This involved a former slave, called Joseph Knight, who had been brought from Jamaica to Scotland by his owner James Wedderburn. The story of Joseph Knight formed the basis of the recent (2004) book by James Robertson.

Knight had run away from Wedderburn, and when he had been found he filed a claim which ended at the Court of Session to protect him from becoming re-enslaved — claiming either freedom or wages for his service.

Dundas' representation was assisted by Samuel Johnson and James Boswell, and the case was heard by the enlightenment writer Henry Home, Lord Kames.

The decision given by Lord Kames was in favour of Joseph Knight, stating that:

> *'the dominion assumed over this Negro, under the law of Jamaica, being unjust, could not be supported in this country to any extent: That, therefore, the defender [Wedderburn] had no right to the Negro's service for any space of time, nor to send him out of the country against his consent.'*

This decision effectively underlined the lack of basis in Scots law for either slavery or 'perpetual service'. That is, although slavery might be legal in Jamaica it was not in Scotland.

7. In office he had a strong impact on the development of the United Kingdom, both in strengthening the union between Scotland and England and also in incorporating Ireland into the UK

Dundas' political career began in the shadow of the Jacobite uprisings of 1715 and 1745, which had both caused considerable strain on the newly created union of the United Kingdom (from 1707). British rule had been forced on Scotland in the wake of the 1745 rebellion, and in the 1770s there were still few Scots in London and even less holding any influence.

Despite this, Dundas refused to become Anglicised when he moved to London, and kept his strong accent throughout his political career.

He also became well known for his patronage of Scots in his appointments, particularly with respect to the building up of British influence in India.

As Lord Rosebery once put it, he Scotticised India, and Orientalised Scotland.

And as Dundas' biographer Furber commented,

> *'there was scarcely a gentleman's family in Scotland, of whatever politics, that had not at some time received some Indian appointment or some act of kindness from Dundas.'*

In 1821, years after the death of Dundas Walter Scott described the Board of Control (of India) as 'the Corn Chest for Scotland, where we poor gentry must send our younger sons, as we send our black cattle to the South.'

One very significant part of Dundas' power base (and hence the power of the Pitt government he was part of for so many years) was his dominance of Scottish politics. He had an extraordinary ability to manage the connections and levers of patronage in the political system of Scotland, and thus the members of parliament who were elected to Westminster.

Dundas became known as the 'political manager of Scotland', or otherwise as the 'Grand Manager of Scotland', or even the 'uncrowned king of Scotland', Harry the Ninth.

His position in London was well recognised in Scotland, to the extent that when riots occurred across the country in 1792, it was effigies of Dundas that were burnt in Perth and Edinburgh, and not of the Prime Minister Pitt.

When Dundas left public office in the 1800s, there is no doubt that not only the state of Britain as a whole, and the union of England and Scotland were much more secure than they had been at the time that he had become involved with national politics. This is not to say that Scotland had in itself benefitted from Dundas' leading position, but certainly much of the nobility of Scotland had been given new opportunities to prosper and succeed in the new ventures of empire that came about in the wake of the loss of the American colonies and the opening up of new colonies and influence in the east.

Alongside this, Dundas also oversaw the union of Ireland into the United Kingdom in 1800. Unlike the mainstream viewpoint, Dundas sought to implement the inclusion of Irish Catholics within the newly established polity, which made him unpopular for a while in both London and Scotland. He was not successful in this respect, particularly due to opposition by King George III, and so the creation of the United Kingdom of Great Britain and Ireland had embedded within it the marginalisation of the majority of the Irish population.

8. Whilst in office he oversaw the challenges of the French Revolution and the rise in Europe of an expanding France under Emperor Napoleon

The two decades in which he was at the centre of government were a time of major transformation in Europe. It was a time when the industrial revolution began, with significant population shifts and changes in the way in which labour was organised.

It also saw in 1789 the French Revolution, which caused significant fears in the UK of similar threats to the establishment, aristocracy, and monarchy. As Home Secretary, Dundas held a substantial responsibility to forestall the movement towards revolution, and to put down public demonstrations that support the French Revolution.

In the aftermath of the revolution, France saw the rise of Napoleon Bonaparte, and his expansion across Europe. This brought the UK directly into war with France for much of two decades, as the two vied for ultimate dominance of Europe and the colonies of Asia.

Dundas had an active role in the management of this war, as War Secretary from 1794 to 1801 often quite unsuccessfully — and he developed a historical reputation for making poor military decisions.

However, Dundas did recognise the importance to British interests of the control of Egypt – before Napoleon launched his invasion – as well as the need to control the African cost, particularly Cape Town to maintain British interests in India.

In 1804, on becoming First Lord of the Admiralty, Dundas made radical changes to the structures and policies of the navy that led to the building of 168 new ships in the space of a single year — which enabled Nelson to win the battle of Trafalgar in 1805.

9. He had a profound impact on the development of the 'Second British Empire' in Asia, including India, Malaya (the Straits of Malacca), and Australia

Following the independence of the US, Dundas largely led the British development of its interests in India. He immersed himself in the detail of the administration of India, which was something no other political figure of his time took the trouble to do. This made his insight the one that largely commanded the British political development of Indian as a new imperial project to replace what it had lost to the United States.

Dundas's vision was one in which there was less emphasis on colonisation and settlement, which he saw as the main problem in America — since the settlers had learnt to see themselves as something other than British.

Instead, he saw the colonial project in India as one of economic exploitation for the sake of British interests — hence the relatively low levels of British settlement and the use of local labour and resources as required.

Dundas also oversaw British control over the important Straits of Malacca which led to China and the spice islands — through the acquisition of Prince Edward Island (now Penang), which was the precursor of Singapore.

Furthermore, he also oversaw British overseas interests during the time of the initial settlement of Australia, particularly the development of new colonies that included the penal colony of Botany Bay.

10. By overseeing the takeover of South Africa in 1795, Dundas established the British rule in the region that eventually became the apartheid system of the twentieth century

In his passion for British expansion in India and other parts of Asia, Dundas also strongly advocated the importance of British interests in the area of South Africa, particularly of Cape Town. He saw this as a vital strategic link in the development of the Asian empire. He oversaw the British takeover of Cape Town from the Dutch in 1795, and he ensured that it remained under British control after it was taken back from the French in 1806.

Indeed he called it his 'favourite child'.

In effect, the political entity that became twentieth century South Africa was largely established under Dundas' oversight. Although for years British rule gave franchise to black African voters, but British rule also brought with it the colonial ideas of (what was considered) scientific racial difference.

Thus it was under British rule in the nineteenth century that the racist establishment was built up that became formalised as apartheid when South Africa took independence in the early twentieth century.

In many respects we can say if there had been no Dundas then there would not have been the need for Nelson Mandela.

11. He coined the word 'starvation' much to the amusement of his classically educated contemporaries in parliament

Dundas is even credited with inventing the word 'starvation', when he used the neologism in a speech on the American war of independence in 1775, much to the amusement of the Latin classicists.

Indeed for a number of years, the term 'starvation' was regularly used by his political opponents to taunt him — he gained the nickname 'starvation Dundas'

He refused to modify his Scots accent for the London political village, dominated by English. Apart from his obvious love of politics he refused to take up too many English ways — except for developing a strong taste for English beer.

Conclusion

There are indeed many reasons to dislike Dundas.

In particular, he left Scotland a mixed legacy often known as 'Dundas Despotism', due to his skilled political management of the system. In many respects, he built a power base on manipulation but also had the effect of paving the way for the later reforms

But the things he did, and the role that he had, are also reasons to remember him, rather than to forget him.

He was an extremely influential figure in British politics during his time, and we should remember such figures for what they have done, and for the impact they have had on our history, for better or worse.

We do not need to glorify them, nor should we judge them too much according to the values of our own age rather than the one they lived in.

In retrospect, it is clear that the ending of the horrific practice of slavery was a necessity during the time of Dundas, and we can either celebrate the fact that he supported the legislation to do so — or condemn him for allowing it to continue for a further 15 years, at the cost primarily of the people who were shipped from Africa to America during that time.

It is questionable whether there is need for the 140 feet high column in St Andrews Square to bring this figure to our attention. But the column is there, and it is a long standing part of the skyline of Edinburgh.

Perhaps a companion memorial should be added to it, to help us also remember the millions of Africans whose lives were ruined by the inhumanity of the slave trade. Although slavery was distant from Scotland, in the Caribbean, it impacted in many ways on Scotland — as shown by the ambiguity of Dundas' own life in this respect.

Chapter 12

Scotland's #Indyref: some historic reflections on Devo-max and independence from Britain

Published in the Huffington Post[37]

9 September 2014

In September 1774, on the eve of the American Revolution, the First Continental Congress met in Philadelphia to discuss the grievances of the 'Thirteen Colonies' against their British rulers. This congress would meet for a second time a few months later, and from it developed the government of the independent United States of America.

One of the representatives at this initial September 1774 meeting was Joseph Galloway, a loyalist to British rule, who later fought on the British side in the war of independence. Galloway put forward to the Congress his Plan of Union[38], which envisaged a framework for the continuance of British rule over the Thirteen American Colonies. This would include a Grand Council or parliament for the Colonies (subject to the power of the British parliament and crown, in its own words 'an inferior and distinct branch of the British legislature'), and a President-General.

In sum, Galloway's plan was largely one of unionist devolution for the American Colonies remaining under British rule. In many respects, this was the 'Devo-Max' option of the American Revolution. For Galloway, the

---

[37] http://www.huffingtonpost.co.uk/malory-nye/devomax-scottish-independence_b_5786102.html
[38] http://press-pubs.uchicago.edu/founders/documents/v1ch7s3.html

American Colonies and Great Britain were better together.

Galloway's Plan of Union was narrowly rejected by the Congress, with a difference of five in favour and six against (out of a total congress of 56). By far the majority of the representatives at that First Continental Congress wished to address their grievances against British rule with a move to independence.

Scotland and the United Kingdom

Scotland in 2014 is, of course, in a very different situation to the USA in 1774. It is notable, however, that the move to American independence was in large part fuelled by the issue of taxation, which has echoes with the rise of Scottish Nationalism in the 1980s under Thatcher's Poll Tax. Indeed, in many respects the establishment of the Scottish Parliament in 1999 is remarkably similar to the structure outlined in Galloway's proposed Plan of Union to the First Congress.

However, we should also remember that when the USA declared independence in 1776, the independence that the new country sought was from the United Kingdom of Great Britain. That is, a country that was made up of both England and Scotland.

Indeed, as Linda Colley points out, one of the grievances of John Adams (later to succeed George Washington to become the 2nd President of the USA) was that:

> '...*The two realms of England and Scotland were, by the Act of Union [1707] incorporated into one kingdom by the name of Great Britain; but there is not one word about America in that Act*' (see Linda Colley, Britons, p.136)

As some may argue (such as Richard Halloran recently), Scotland is the last of the English colonies to leave the fold, and the vote on 18 September may possibly be the final end of the long decline of the British Empire.

If this is the case (or at least partially), we also must remember that the United Kingdom will still remain intact (albeit without Scotland), and the Principality of Wales will still remain in the political partnership with England — and also Northern Ireland, of course.

The comparison with American Independence does also draw our attention to the fact that the United Kingdom has a long history of ceding power. In fact, this has been happening for much of its history as a united kingdom.

A long history of independences from Britain

When the Act of Union between Scotland and England came about in 1707, the new United Kingdom of Great Britain ruled over a substantial empire that included 13 American Colonies (although Georgia was not founded as a colony at that time, the colony of Carolina was divided into North and South until 1729).

The loss of the American colonies was a blow to Scotland as well as to England. But history tells us that the loss of that empire was balanced very quickly by new gains for Great Britain.

Indeed, the combination of Scotland and England as the United Kingdom proved a very potent force. The American colonies were no longer under their rule, but Britain's substantial global power continued — with Canadian and Caribbean colonies in full strength, together with the newly emerging eastern empire in Asia (particularly India).

The nation's recovery in the last part of the eighteenth century, and the subsequent development of the Second British Empire (after American Independence), was largely due to Scotland and England working together. This came about, for example, in the income generated by Scottish and English owned slave plantations in the Caribbean, and also the highly successful political alliance between William Pitt (the younger) and the Scottish politician, Henry Dundas (see Furber). And it was a united British (English and Scottish) army that defeated Napoleon at Waterloo (with help from the Germans), and cemented Britain's role in the nineteenth century as the primary European superpower.

The end of the nineteenth century, along with the first half of the twentieth, saw this change substantially. During that time Britain began to see the long process of colonies again move towards and achieve independence across the empire. Canada between 1867 and 1931, Australia between 1901 and 1939, New Zealand between 1907 and 1947, Ireland in 1921, India and Pakistan in 1947, Malaysia in 1957, and the African nations in the 1960s. One of the exceptions to this process was, of course, Hong Kong, which in 1997 did not take independence from Britain, but instead underwent the transfer of rule from Britain to China, under the terms of the leases signed by the two countries in the late nineteenth century.

Great Britain has become very familiar with the process of granting independence to territories under its sovereignty. Unfortunately, however, it has been quite rare for this to occur peacefully and without conflict.

Is it now better for Scotland to be separate from Britain?

The question that Scotland is now facing is to what extent have Scotland and England been irretrievably integrated by this shared process, as Great Britain? Are the two countries like a married couple, as parents of several generations of children who have all now grown up and flown the nest (USA, Canada, Australia, Ireland, India, etc.)? Or is it more true to say that England has been a harsh patriarch who has sought the subjugation of all under his control — including Scotland?

The Better Together campaign has been stressing with great clarity the benefits of the English-Scottish partnership, as before did the British loyalists to their American subjects in the 1770s. It is true that there have been many benefits to Scotland of rule from Westminster in the past 300 plus years — not least Scotland being able to exercise international power (and accumulate considerable wealth) through the UK in a way that it could not have done on its own.

The impact of Scottish independence might not be as significant in the long term as what happened in America in 1776. Its local impact, however, will be immense — particularly in terms of what will happen to the remainder of the United Kingdom after Scotland's departure.

It is interesting even to ask whether there can be a United Kingdom of Great Britain once Scotland has left, since such an entity has only existed since 1707, including Scotland. Prior to 1707 the union of England and Wales was known simply as the Kingdom of England, following Henry the Eighth's incorporation of the Welsh legal system into England in 1535.

As I have argued elsewhere, Scotland will not stop being British after independence (see chapter four) . Being 'British' will remain as a regional identity for Scots (akin to being Scandinavian in the Nordic countries), even if or when Scots cease to have a default British national citizenship.

For over three hundred years Scotland has had a very significant impact on world history, as a prominent partner within the United Kingdom. This has been both positive and negative. The partnership has given us the

Scottish Enlightenment, has powered the industrial revolution, and Scottish science, creativity, and knowledge continue to pack a considerable punch in today's world.

However, Scots also took their share of the spoils and exploitations of empire. The country achieved great wealth through the ownership and abuse of slaves, and many prominent Scots oversaw and led the development of the British Empire. This was all achieved through Scotland being part of the economic and political partnership of the United Kingdom.

There is now a very distinct possibility that Scotland may vote on 18 September to change this partnership. I am intrigued about what further this country has in store, quite possibly as an independent nation in its own right.

Unlike the options given to the American colonies, it is good to have the chance to do this through a vote.

It really is a historic opportunity.

Part Four

Getting ready for the #Indyref, September 2014

Chapter 13

The issue with Scottish independence is not 'Yes' or 'No': it is *when* and *how*

Published in the Huffington Post[39]

15 September 2014

Is this the time to say 'the Time is Now'?

There shall be an independent Scotland. There should be no doubt about this.

The issue is no longer about 'Yes' or 'No'.

It is about how and when.

It is still not clear if this is the right time or not. But even if the decision on 18 September is 'No', the momentum for change is now too strong. As the Conservative Scottish Secretary Michael Forsyth[40] once said about devolution, 'humpty dumpty cannot be put back together'.

Although Scotland and England have both benefitted substantially from their three hundred year old partnership, the world is now a different place.

If there is one thing that has emerged from this referendum debate, it is the realisation that many people in Scotland — a number that is close to a majority — now have considerable doubts about the future of the current mode of partnership between Scotland and the other members of the

---

[39] http://www.huffingtonpost.co.uk/malory-nye/scottish-independence-_b_5816578.html
[40] http://www.huffingtonpost.co.uk/malory-nye/ukip-election-diversity_b_5394771.html

British union. As George Monbiot has argued so well, if the choice was for an independent Scotland to be joining such a union, it is very unlikely that the majority would vote to go in.

The decision will therefore be based on the old Newtonian equation of momentum versus inertia. Perhaps this may be the case of the unstoppable meeting the immovable.

For a long time I have thought that the timing of the Scottish independence referendum was not good. I do strongly believe that Scottish independence will happen someday, but I am not sure if it will happen in my lifetime.

My sense was that it was too soon to schedule the vote for autumn 2014, just fifteen years after the re-establishment of the Scottish parliament. I did not think that the Scottish people were quite ready for the leap of faith (and hope) that was needed for an independent nation.

I still have my doubts about the outcome this month. Despite all the weaknesses so far of the 'Better Together' campaign, we cannot underestimate the power of caution, a fear of what sacrifices might need to be made perhaps for the 'luxury' of independence. This is not only the matter of the pound, it is about a much deeper fear of the precariousness of recovery. It is possible that the irrelevance to Scotland of the housing bubble in south east England — together with the promises of becoming an oil-rich economy — may address these fears.

It is certain that the 'Yes' campaign has won the battle that matters most in the long term. That is the battle on social media, particularly on Twitter. The tweets may be short and ephemeral, but that is now the domain where, more than anywhere else, the opinions and values of the future are being built (the 'Generation Yes'). However, the wider battle — particularly at the ballot box — is probably a harder one to win.

I have made bad calls before on voting. In summer and autumn 2008 I felt in my bones that the US electorate would not bring themselves to vote for an African American president. I was happily wrong on that, and then they did it again in 2012.

America had at that time the memory of Bush to motivate them. For us in Scotland, it is Cameron, and the long historical shadow of Margaret Thatcher.

Part of me now thinks that an independent Scotland might come into being on 24 March 2016. Why not?

For many it is simply the case that the 'Time is Now'. Others are still asking themselves the question, is it now, is this the time?

What will not be clear until 19 September is whether this is strong enough to reach the tipping point of real change. I don't yet feel I am living in a country, surrounded by people, who are thrilled to have the chance to throw off the chains from a foreign power. I would like to feel that Scotland is in the midst of its own velvet (oatcake?) revolution, like Hungary and Czechoslovakia in 1989 — or Slovakia in 1993.

Maybe that sense of hope, anticipation, and national destiny will come about after the decision has been made. 18 September will only be a starting point, after all.

Of course, a 'No' vote can be reversed sometime in the future — as happened with the devolution referendums of 1979 and 1997. If the vote is 'No' there will remain a significant minority who wish to see independence. However, a 'Yes' vote for independence will be pretty damn irreversible (as many unionists are now reminding us). A vote for 'Yes' will bring in changes that are not likely to be revisited this century.

Needless to say, this long term issue is profoundly significant. The vote will decide on the political make-up of the country that my children grow up, mature, and live their adult lives in. This may be as part of the United Kingdom, or in an independent Scotland, with a Scottish passport.

I can't help asking myself 'what right do I have to make that decision for them?' But it is my responsibility to do so, at least for those who do not have the vote themselves. And it is my responsibility to vote in a way that does justice to their potential.

There is no doubt that Scotland can be a successful independent country. No doubt at all.

We cannot say, and never will know, which of the two options would be better for us — since in choosing one over the other the decision is made, and the history is decided.

Ten or twenty years from now we may look back and regret the decision, either thinking of the wasted opportunity for independence, or regretting making a rash decision which resulted in a lower living standard for those north of the border. Fear of making the wrong decision is a powerful force, but we cannot know which one is 'wrong' before we make it.

According to Alasdair Douglas[41], a Scot who chairs the City of London

Law Society, one the main beneficiaries of independence will be the lawyers. Constitutional change is always a costly matter, and this will drill down to legal changes at the micro level. Perhaps students at law school will be the crucial demographic group who influence the decision in the end?

We are hearing now the convincing argument that independence will protect Scotland from the Ukip agenda — that is the prospect of an exit from the EU. How would Scotland feel if (remaining in the UK) they went on to vote also to stay in the EU, but had to leave due to a majority in England voting for an exit? Despite the fears raised about an independent Scotland being vetoed from EU membership, there is now a stronger likelihood of Scotland remaining in the EU as an independent nation, rather than as part within the UK.

We must always remember that the United Kingdom is not such an ancient institution that it cannot change. The UK as we now know it came about in 1707 through an Act of Union (largely on England's terms), but Scotland has prospered from that union during much that history, particularly through the joint endeavour of the British Empire.

But that does not mean the continuance of the union is historically inevitable. And many other countries that were in partnership with England (and the UK) have now gone their own way. Very few would now say that Australia, New Zealand, Canada, or even the USA would be 'better together' with the UK.

The prospect of independence in Scotland is seemingly taking hold of the country's imagination at last (or at least a sizable proportion). It is not every day that we have the chance to bring about the peaceful division of the United Kingdom to create a new nation for an ancient people.

It has also been rare for such nationalism to be inclusive and multicultural. Indeed, the backwardness appears to be more pronounced on the other side, with those who wish Scotland to remain wedded to a narrow form of British nationalism.

However, we should not kid ourselves. An independent Scotland is not going to be a kinder, gentler, nicer place to live. Our politicians will continue to be self-serving, even though they do that in Edinburgh rather than London. And of course, many of the current unionists who are

---

[41] http://www.lawgazette.co.uk/law/city-leader-warns-of-legal-dangers-of-scottish-yes-vote/5042044.article

warning us of the dire consequences of independence will eventually come round to the idea of serving their country in Holyrood rather than Westminster. Independence will just make them that bit closer, and hopefully put them in a more functional (and less archaic and anachronistic) system.

This will not be the end of being British, it will just make it a regional identity rather than the basis of a national citizenship.

I feel in my bones that perhaps, yes quite maybe, that the time is now right to say *The Time is Now*, the time for Scotland to take charge of ourselves.

A once in a lifetime opportunity for peaceful independence for Scotland should not be missed.

Chapter 14

While Cameron pleads for us to keep it in the family, Scotland sings 'I want to break free'...

Published in the Huffington Post[42]

17 September 2014

When I first got married back in 1985 (just a few years after Prince Charles and Diana), most of my friends went to great lengths to ask me if I was concerned about the fact that 'one in three marriages end in divorce'. At the time I felt it was a strange thing to ask a soon-to-be newly-wed, and I simply shrugged it off. History in those past thirty years has told us that even the marriages of the great and good (including royals) can end in tears and break-ups, and new found independence.

David Cameron took the trouble to fly up to Aberdeen last night (15 September) and asked me to consider the union between Scotland and England (and Wales and Northern Ireland) as a sort of marriage. I am a Scottish voter, and so I presume I was one of the people he was addressing.

He outlined[43] this vision of the 'Great Britain' family:

---

[42] http://www.huffingtonpost.co.uk/malory-nye/scottish-independence_b_5827918.html

[43] http://www.huffingtonpost.co.uk/2014/09/15/david-cameron-warns-of-a-painful-divorce-if-scotland-votes-for-independence_n_5823692.html?utm_hp_ref=uk-politics&ir=UK+Politics

THERE SHALL BE AN INDEPENDENT SCOTLAND

'This is a decision that could break up our family of nations, and rip Scotland from the rest of the UK.

'Scotland, England, Wales and Northern Ireland, different nations, with individual identities competing with each other even at times enraging each other while still being so much stronger together. We are a family of nations.'

It was an interesting metaphor to use in the context. If we think that he could have chosen any form of rhetoric, he could have emphasised an economic or rational case for continuing the partnership. His choice was instead to put the relationship in very personal, and indeed gendered terms. He took the role of the wounded husband, pleading with his wife to stay together 'for the sake of the kids' and for 'all that we've been through'. After all:

'...we built this home together.'

But as with Cameron's Britain, families are largely shaped by power, and the functionality of the family is the product of how that power is exercised.

A family is rarely based on egalitarianism, in most cases there are one or more dominant members, usually the parents. From the reports of Cameron's speech, it is not quite clear in this case exactly 'who is the daddy?'. But in the long 'family' history there is one member whose behaviour has been of particular concern. England has always been the dominant partner, as evidenced most obviously by the location of the Parliament and central government of this 'family of nations'.

However, for Cameron

'A family is not a compromise, or a second best, it is a magical identity, that makes us more together than we can ever be apart, so please — do not break this family apart.'

The optimistic vision is of our family of nations staying together, there for each other in the hard times, coming through to better times.

What Cameron failed to say, however, is that in modern Britain the odds of a successful marriage have drifted out even further than they were in my youth. According to the Office of National Statistics, the data from the 2013 census in England and Wales now shows 42% of marriages ending in divorce.

As we are all truly aware, divorce is now mainstream — almost as many marriages fail as succeed.

On top of that, of course, there is the issue of what takes place within the family itself. For many, the family is a safe and loving social unit (the 'magical entity'), even if it is eventually soured by divorce.

But we should not forget the fact that the family may often be the location of violence and abuse, particularly directed by the dominant (usually male) partner against the other (usually female) partner and their children.

According to Women's Aid[44] in 2011/12

> '31% women and 18% men have experienced domestic abuse since the age of 16 years.
> 'This amounts to 5 million women and 2.9 million men...
> 'In 2011/12, the police reported nearly 800,000 incidents of domestic violence.
> 'On average 2 women a week are killed by a male partner or former partner: this constitutes around one-third of all female homicide victims.
> 'There are around 500,000 victims of sexual assault each year, 85%-90% of whom are women.
> 56% [of the perpetrators of the most serious sexual offences against women] were partners/ex-partners.'

And according to the NSPCC[45], in 2011

> 'Five per cent of under 11s, 13.4 per cent of 11-17s and 14.5 per cent of 18-24s had experienced severe maltreatment [including sexual abuse] by a parent or guardian during their childhood.'

---

[44] http://www.womensaid.org.uk/core/core_picker/download.asp?id=1602

[45] http://www.nspcc.org.uk/Inform/research/findings/child_abuse_neglect_research_wda84173.html

So where does that leave Cameron's emotional appeal to the magical 'family of nations'?

Is the United Kingdom a 'Disney family', with its ups and down, but where all-will-be-well before the credits role at the end?

Or is it something closer to the abusive or dysfunctional reality that exists outside of this nostalgic bubble?

It is important, of course, to remember that the act of saying a family is loving and happy does not mean it necessarily is. And quite obviously if one of the partners is on the verge of 'walking out the door' (to use Cameron's own phrase) there is clearly something going wrong.

It is hard to avoid the metaphor of England (that largest and most populous nation of the United Kingdom, and therefore the 'dominant' partner) as an abusive husband and father. This is not necessarily the case, but there are strong grievances in Scotland (and in other places) that the relationship has not been (and still is not) a positive or healthy one.

There is no simple narrative here — the experience of being Scottish in the United Kingdom is extremely varied. We can do no justice to that by trying to simplify it to the extreme of saying we are one big happy family.

Most chillingly Cameron warned that

'Independence would not be a trial separation, it would be a painful divorce.'

The separating out of Scotland from the United Kingdom will not be an easy process. The warning is that (like an awkward ex) England would make that process as difficult as possible.

Many of us have been there, done that, and wondered if it was worth it. Only to remember that the painful divorce was the less bad option, it was the alternative to staying in a more painful marriage.

And that is perhaps the biggest weakness of Cameron's argument. We should no longer assume that divorce is the 'nuclear' option. Divorce is the mainstream. We are used to living with families that are separated and blended.

And most of us are thankful that abused wives and children are no longer obliged to put up with the abusive father, as would have been the only option in the 1950s family Cameron is pointing us back to.

If we want to see our national politics in familial terms, then we should feel quite alright about doing it in a twenty-first century manner. No divorce is painless, but very often it is what the individuals want.

In truth, if the 18 September vote has a 'Yes' majority, and Scotland chooses for itself to 'leave' the family of Great Britain, it will do so as a young adult seeking their own independence, and not because of any marital breakdown.

That is in itself an emotional time for all involved, but the family is not 'broken' by the change. Scotland will remain part of Britain, and England should learn to live more easily with itself and its grown up 'family'.

Part Five

After the #Indyref
There shall be an independent Scotland

Chapter 15

The day after yesterday (the day after the referendum)

20 September 2014

April 10, 1992 was a dark and depressing day in Scotland. In the General Election the day before the country had not voted in a single Conservative MP, and yet it was to face five more years of a Conservative Government. The Thatcher years of the 1980s had been too much to bear already.

For myself and more than a million and a half other residents of Scotland, today is an equally bad day. We had the chance as a country to do something different, and we didn't take it. At least, not enough of us took it.

The majority of the two million voters who chose 'No' did not do so to keep the Tory coalition in place. But that is the result. They have made Cameron a happier man. He now only has to find a way to fudge his promises of 'greater powers'.

I believe that, in fact, very few politicians have come out well from the referendum. Probably most kudos will go to Gordon Brown, for saying the things that Scots wanted to hear — when would things be done, what were the choices that needed to be made? Other than that, the Better Together campaign was an exercise in how to make falling of a log as difficult as possible, whilst the Yes campaign did all the right things apart from the win the vote.

There is no doubt that the movement to independence has come a very long way. The SNP took us into this referendum with no reasonable prospect of winning it, and so it was a significant triumph in itself that nearly half the electorate were expecting victory. In the longer term, the pledges of devo-max that were wrung out of the ruling elite at Westminster will most likely be enough to move on the cause of Scottish nationalism for this generation.

My expectation remains, however, that Scottish will one day be independent.

This is not because of Scottish dislike of the United Kingdom, or a lack of commonality between Scots and other Britons. Regardless of the outcome of the #Indyref, Scotland would have continued to have close ties with England, Wales, and Ireland.

But there continues to be a strong inclination towards independence, most clearly evidenced by the substantial numbers voting 'Yes'.

This is about more than nationalism. As I have discussed earlier (in chapter 3), national identity can be ambiguous, and is often much more than a simple binary between Britishness and Scottishness. After all, English national identity has played a significant part in the #Indyref debates (among Westminster politicians at least), and the strength of British nationalism has largely been left unnoticed.

One problem with many of the debates in the lead up to the referendum is that the focus has been too much on the binary, either one form of nationalism or the other. This was a two way contest in the end, with either the UK nation remaining intact or a new Scottish nation-state re-emerging. But for most of those voting, the issues were more blurred, with their sense of nationalism and identity going both ways.

My initial thought is that having succeeded beyond expectations, the necessity is for the SNP to adapt and learn from this successful defeat. It has grown and changed considerably over the years of devolution – largely through the leadership of Alex Salmond. But it is out of touch in some ways, as evidenced in particular by the disparity between the SNP's political heartlands and the areas where the Yes vote was strongest. Dundee was the exception to this, but otherwise, it appears that the Yes vote was largely among Labour voters rather than the SNP.

The move to independence is about more than nationalism and it is much more than the SNP. To make it happen sooner rather than later, there needs to be a broad 'rainbow' alliance that goes across and beyond political parties. This is what worked for the Yes campaign. The SNP on its own will not be able to deliver what the people of Scotland want.

And so we must all learn from this defeat, and we must try to take the longer historical view. Clearly this was not the time, the change will be evolutionary rather than revolutionary. We have come a long way in just twenty years, from centralisation to devolution, and from there to whatever devo-max may be offered.

This is certainly onwards and upwards, perhaps. At a snail's pace, but at least it is in the right direction.

So what can we learn from this exercise in democracy?

The astonishing turnout of the vote across Scotland has shown us that elections really do matter, particularly when people are given a chance to see that they matter. For too many people, for most of the time, elections are about parties that all seem to be the same, even when they are not. Politicians and commentators need to move from bemoaning that fact to looking for ways to harness the power of democracy more effectively.

That does not happen every time, but when it does happen it is a force that can change the world (or at least our small part of it).

Chapter 16

I voted Yes to an independent Scotland… and I look forward to the day when it happens

Published on medium.com[46]

23 September 2014

I voted Yes last week. Like many others in Scotland I was gutted with the result.

I have always felt that I am British. My family origins are in south east England, around London, and I spent my childhood between Essex and rural mid Wales. I have lived much of my adult life in Scotland.

If Scotland had become an independent country I do not know if I would have taken up a Scottish passport or stayed as a UK citizen.

But I still felt passionately that it was right to vote Yes.

Me and 1.6 million other people.

A small number of people did this for narrow, small minded, petty nationalist reasons. There were xenophobes, English haters, and other general nasties – but no more so than can be found in any group of people. There were similar nasties in the 'No' voting group, as evidenced by the disturbances in George Square in Glasgow on Friday night. The nasties did not define the attraction of the Yes movement for an independent Scotland.

---

[46] http://medium.com/@malorynye/i-voted-yes-to-an-independent-scotland-85c278680ca0 http://medium.com/@malorynye/i-voted-yes-to-an-independent-scotland-85c278680ca0

The basis of 'the 45' (percent) vote was hope and respect, not hatred or fear.

It was not about the break up of the United Kingdom or about a dislike of English people. To put it simply, when an adult child wants to leave home and set up on their own, it is not because they hate their parents, it is simply that they feel the time is right for them look after themselves.

The Yes vote was a gesture of self-confidence, about the desire to make this small part of Europe and the British Isles a place that can work on its own terms.

To my regret, this was not shared by enough people to win the day. We have not been given the chance to show how well an independent Scotland could get on with our brothers and sisters in the rest of Britain.

But this is not the end of the story. We are clear that this was a once in a generation opportunity for Scotland. Both Cameron and Salmond have ruled out the possibility of the referendum being repeated soon.

Even so, the desire for this change will not disappear in Scotland. The thunderingly loud call of 1.6 million people cannot be easily ignored or brushed aside.

Scotland will one day be independent, just as other countries such as Canada, Australia, and New Zealand have become independent from the UK.

For that to happen, there is clearly a lot more work that needs to be done. It will not happen on its own.

Scotland will achieve independence when it feels it is the right time. Obviously this was not the time.

There was too much fear and caution. Economic fear (very understandable after the years of recession, and the turbulence of the international markets) and caution about the unknown steps that needed to be taken.

The other path, the one offered by the 'No' supporters was equally unknown. It will take us along a route that is very different from where we have been before, but it looked more familiar and so seemed more safe and secure.

When the time is right for independence, these opposites will be reversed. Independence will be the attractive and seemingly secure path to take. When that happens, the independence movement will need to offer a future that we feel we know and understand. We will have to learn ways in which that can come about.

But an independent Scotland will happen one day.

Chapter 17

'Dear Generation Yes'
an open letter to the new generation who hoped for Scottish independence

Published on medium.com[47]

20 September 2014

It will happen one day, thanks to you…

This is a time when you will feel the hurt.

But despite the outcome of the referendum you have been part of a historic event, a momentous change. Even if it was not yet the change you had been hoping for.

Because of the pain and disappointment it worth taking the trouble to look back in history a little, to see how far we have come to be here at this point.

It might seem to you that 1997 was a long time ago. For many in Generation Yes it was around the time you born. That was when we had the 11/9 referendum, the 'Yes/Yes' vote, that saw the establishment of the Scottish Parliament. Until it happened, few people had dared hoped to see the day.

We remember the despair of the years before, particularly on 10 April 1992, when not a single Conservative MP was elected in Scotland, but we still had the prospect of another five years of Tory power in Westminster. Any form of 'home rule' in Scotland at that time seemed like an impossible

---

[47] http://medium.com/@malorynye/dear-generation-yes-an-open-letter-to-the-new-generation-who-hoped-for-scottish-independence-8797504a6d6f

dream.

But on 11 September 1997, just five years later, we had the chance to make that change. We were able to deliver our votes to create our parliament. The Scottish Parliament that we now take for granted. The Parliament that many were sceptical about, that Billy Connolly worried would turn out as a 'wee pretendy parliament'.

This Parliament is not everything that it could and should be. But it has given us the chance to make laws for ourselves, preserve the NHS, keep free university tuition fees, protect our vulnerable, and pursue a society based on social justice.

This is the Parliament that enabled us to have the 2014 Referendum on independence. And it has changed the voting age for the referendum (and hopefully will do so for all elections) to 16, so you could have your say.

The Parliament is still young, it has much work to do. And hopefully it will become more powerful now.

So remember how it was born out of the despair and despondency of 1992, out of a time when no one thought they would ever see that day.

And remember also how far we have come from there.

Scottish independence used to be the dream of the few, of a minority of a minority. It was seen as the pursuit of the idealists and the fringes. Even when the Scottish Nationalist Party first formed a government in 2007, they were seen as winning despite their agenda for independence, not because of it.

When the movement for the referendum first went forward in 2011 there were few people who thought there would be any chance of it being successful.

Scottish independence is now mainstream. Don't be fooled into thinking it was 'only' 45%.

It was 45% who said they wanted a new independent Scotland, in a referendum that could have led to that change. I would not have believed that possible just a few years ago.

Now anything is possible.

You were given a vote this time and you used it wisely and responsibly. Those of us in the older generations gave great thought to you, as you will one day inherit the leadership of this country. We want it to be a country you are proud of and that gives you every opportunity to prosper and succeed.

There shall be an independent Scotland, one day.

The question really is how and why. If we give thought to that, then the Yes will be delivered.

We must learn from the fears of our fellows, why they did not feel that this was the time to make the change.

What is it about the union that they wish to keep, and what is it about independence that gave them caution? If we can understand those things, then the task of convincing the majority that independence is the best future for Scotland becomes so much easier.

This is a fitting time for you to come into this new landscape of Scotland. Alex Salmond's sad resignation illustrates that the baton is in the process of being passed down to you.

It may take a generation to achieve the goal that we are looking for. For the magic of a Yes vote that takes us past the 50% tipping point. It may happen sooner.

But what will make that happen is for you to apply yourself, use the role model of Salmond to see how to take an idea out from the wilderness into the mainstream. We can all do this in our own way.

We can all help to take the mainstream idea of independence and make it so compelling that the majority want it. Not just an uneasy 55%, but a comfortable 60 or 70%.

It is about many things, pride in our nation, economic security, social justice, reassurance about our relations with our neighbours and the wider world, and much more besides.

Just as in 1997 the idea of a Parliament was unstoppable and uncontroversial, we can similarly work together to make the idea of independence the most secure and viable option for our future – without the room for doubt and fear.

To do this we can and should work together. As Salmond has said, this is about far more than a single person, or a single party. The SNP have been the catalyst, but the Yes Campaign mobilised people and ideas from across the country.

The cause of independence needs a rainbow alliance that continues onwards and upwards from the 45% on 18 September 2014. People of all parties should be part of this, as well as those who have don't want to give allegiance to any.

Together we will do this.

We will achieve independence one day, and create an inclusive, diverse Scotland that is at ease with itself and with our neighbours and friends.

And it is you, Generation Yes, that will make that happen.

Chapter 18

Conclusion: imagine an independent Scotland

The trouble with dust is that it settles and then gets stirred up again, and then settles again, and again and again. Only long-term historical hindsight can tell us what has been buried in the dust and what has succeeded unscathed.

The #Indyref stirred up a lot of dust: the country has changed through going through this process. That dust will not settle in a matter of weeks, or months, or years. Those who say the dust has settled are those who have an interest in maintaining a status quo.

However, none of us are able to stand still.

As I write this conclusion in April 2015, public debates are concentrated on the UK General Election. Most predictions are of a 'hung parliament', with either of the large parties (Conservative and Labour) vying for support from the smaller parties. The predictions also foresee the SNP having a substantial number of MPs (a majority amongst Scottish seats, perhaps nearly all of them) and thus able to support a party of its choice in government.

Much is being made of this in the pre-election frenzy — with many English politicians (on all sides) throwing muck at the SNP's new leader Nicola Sturgeon and her party's policies (and very often her gender). Dire predictions are made that a Labour-SNP alliance (whether formal or informal) will lead inevitably to the 'break up of the Union'.

Who knows what will happen? The result will be dramatic, but most likely in ways that we cannot so easily predict.

If there is such a surge of electoral support for the SNP, then this will in itself be a clear signal of dissatisfaction in Scotland about the outcomes of the #Indyref.

If that does not happen, then a Conservative victory (potentially based on support from Ukip) will take the UK into a further referendum, on British membership of the European Union, which will re-open tensions between the divergent wishes of Scotland and England. Nicola Sturgeon has warned that a vote for the UK to leave the EU may be grounds for a new Scottish independence referendum.

All this will play out in its own particular way.

My own prediction, that I have stated through this book, is that independence will happen at some point. It may take a lot longer than the term of the next UK (or Scottish) parliament. But it will be worth waiting for — even if I am not around to see it.

I am not against British nationalism, nor am I against the UK as a political entity. But neither of these by necessity have to include Scotland, particularly as a significant number of Scots do not want to be part of them.

Britishness is more than a form of nationalism. Being British is part of belonging to a changing culture which has emerged out particular trajectories of histories among the people of this island in north-west Europe. Our various British cultures have areas of overlap and commonality, partly through shared political and national structures, and also largely due to the sharing (to a large extent) of the common *lingua franca* of English. The connections between the different parts of Britain have emerged from generations of interactions, going in all directions. Scotland, England, Wales, and Ireland have truly been mixed up over the last millennium in so many different ways.

Such is the nature of the contemporary world. We all have connections that go far beyond the boundaries of the isles of Britain. We can learn to live with each other quite easily if the border from Carlisle to Berwick becomes an international border. If both Scotland and England both choose to remain in the EU, the border is highly unlikely to change in any significant way.

Whatever happens, things will change. The world is changing, and the pace of change from within and without is much faster than many of us find comfortable. The United Kingdom itself will change, even if it does not disintegrate.

The United Kingdom has been a nation of migration for centuries.

English (and French) influences in Scotland have shaped all three countries in significant ways over the past millennium, as shown perhaps through the examples of the Treaty of Perpetual Peace, the Protestant Reformations, and the union of the crowns.

Scotland and England (and Wales and Ireland) saw extensive outward migrations over the centuries, creating settler colonies in America and elsewhere, transplanting forms of British culture across the world, and in doing so created significant chunks of the modern world. Where the British did not settle they moved other populations — slaves from Africa to the New World, indentured workers from India to Africa and south-east Asia and beyond. This all happened in previous centuries, long before the twentieth century migrations into Britain from these former colonies.

But these latter migrations have happened, and further migrations continue to happen — out of and into Britain — and they will continue. One of the lessons of the early twenty-first century is that successful economies *need* migration (for both 'low' and 'high' end skills). At present the political debates in Scotland seem to have grasped this, whilst English politicians have tended to be more concerned with overcrowding within the particular areas around the English capital of London.

It is blindingly obvious to say that England has transformed in the last century — in the time since the supposed 'golden days' of Downton Abbey. And, of course, Scotland and other parts of the UK have also transformed. And very few people would like to go back to those 'golden days', not even perhaps aristocrats such as David Cameron.

We have no problems imagining that past, what we find more difficult is to imagine the future. And that is where the reality of an independent Scotland will be found. In imagining its reality: of seeing a place that we know and find a home in, even before it has emerged into reality.

It is when we have found that place that there will be an overwhelming vote for Scottish independence.

And it will happen one day, to be sure.

About the author

MALORY NYE is a writer and independent scholar with research interests in the areas of multiculturalism, religious and cultural diversity, and contemporary society.

He is a Research Scholar at the Ronin Institute.

He is the author of three books, including Religion: the Basics, which he is currently revising for its third edition.

He has edited the journal Culture and Religion since 2000, and he blogs on his website, the Huffington Post, and Medium, and he contributes to the Vidoyen expert video site. He is also currently preparing several courses for the online learning platform Udemy.

He has a lifelong passion for the changing landscape of higher eduction, academic life, and the sharing of knowledge. He has recently begun a new podcast series on iTunes titled Religion Bites, together with his podcast Malory Nye: writer & academic.

He lives in Perth, Scotland with his wife and two of his five children.

Learn more about Malory at:

> http://www.amazon.com/Malory-Nye/e/B001HD02CU
> or http://www.amazon.co.uk/Malory-Nye/e/B001HD02CU.

You can also find more details about Malory on his website malorynye.com.

His contact details are:

> email: malory@malorynye.com
> facebook: malorynye
> twitter: @malorynye

Other books by Malory Nye

Religion the Basics
(Routledge, 2nd edition 2008, first edition 2003)

Multiculturalism and Minority Religions in Britain
(RoutledgeCurzon, 2001)

A Place for our Gods
(Curzon, 1996)

Time for Change Report
(Al-Maktoum Institute Academic Press, 2006, co-authored with Abd al-Fattah El-Awaisi)

One last thing...

If you enjoyed this book or found it useful I'd be very grateful if you'd post a short review on Amazon. Your support really does make a difference and I read all the reviews personally so I can get your feedback and make this book even better.

If you'd like to leave a review then all you need to do is click the review link on this book's page on Amazon here:

http://amzn.to/1Hv4nt3

Thanks again for your support!

Printed in Great Britain
by Amazon.co.uk, Ltd.,
Marston Gate.